garden Retreats

garden Retreats

CREATING AN OUTDOOR SANCTUARY

Barbara Blossom Ashmun

PHOTOGRAPHS BY Allan Mandell

CHRONICLE BOOKS

SAN FRANCISCO

Library of Congress Cataloging-in-Publication Data:

Ashmun, Barbara
Garden Retreats / by Barbara Blossom Ashmun and Allan Mandell.
p.   cm.
Includes bibliographical references.
ISBN 0-8118-2500-0 (pbk.)
1. Sanctuary Gardens.   I. Mandell, Allan.   II. Title
SB454.3.S25a75   2000
712'.6—dc21   98-53663
                  CIP
Printed in Hong Kong
Designed and typeset by Bullet Liongson

The photographer wishes to thank: Barbara Ashmun, who has been a
steady light right from the beginning; Betsy Amster, my literary agent;
Mikyla Bruder, Leslie Jonath and the staff of Chronicle Books; and the
benevolent gardeners who so kindly allowed me to photograph the
personal spaces of their gardens. This book is dedicated to those who
have had the experience of spending quiet time in a garden and have
emerged calmer, clearer, more refreshed and revitalized than when they
entered. I hope that more people will slow down and participate in this
valuable activity, and be inspired to create their own garden retreats, if
not on their premises, at least in their hearts.

Distributed in Canada by Raincoast Books
8680 Cambie Street
Vancouver, British Columbia V6P 6M9

10 9 8 7 6 5 4 3 2 1

Chronicle Books
85 Second Street
San Francisco, California 94105

www.chroniclebooks.com

The section "Sitting for the Soul" in chapter seven appeared
in a slightly different form in *Fine Gardening* October 1998.

TABLE OF CONTENTS

ACKNOWLEDGMENTS

Without the garden makers, and the friends who have helped me find them, this book would be no more than an abstract idea. I am grateful to the many talented gardeners who welcomed me into their private sanctuaries and shared their process of discovery and invention. It's been a joy and a privilege to visit so many inspiring retreats, to witness so much creative energy at work.

My deep appreciation to Steven Antonow, Jeffrey Bale, Tess Beistal, Stephen T. Carruthers, Bobbi Feyerabend, Anne-Marie Fischer, Donna and Tony Freeman, Keith Geller, Margaret de Haas van Dorsser and Mark Greenfield, Lucy and Fred Hardiman, Robin Hopper and Judi Dyelle, Cyril Hume, Virginia Israelit, Millie Kiggins, Liz Lair, Stephen Lamphear, Liz Marantz, Laurie McKay, Sue Moss, Lee Neff, Marietta and Ernie O'Byrne, Marti Roberts Pillon, Virginia and Bob Plainfield, John Platt and the late Jane Platt, Rick Pope and Debbie Gorenstein, Elfie Rahr, Marian Raitz, Janet Roberts, Marlene Salon, Marilyn Schultz, Sue Skelly, Bee Smith, Mike Snyder, Stefanie Vancura, Penny Vogel, Nani Waddoups and Ron Wagner, Bruce Wakefield and Jerry Grossnickle, Dotty and Jim Walters, Terry Welch, Chris Keylock Williams and Margaret Willoughby.

I am thankful for all the loving friends, family and instructive mentors who have supported, encouraged and helped me all along the way, especially Betsy Amster, John Benecki, Mikyla Bruder, Ruth Rogers Clausen, Sandy Childress, L. Wendy Dunder, Sarita and Raymond Eisenstark, Becky Gammons, Pamela Harper, Rosie Hamilton, Mary Huey, Trudy Hussman, Leslie Jonath, Peter Joyes, LaVerne Kludsikofsky, Paul Lenz, Allan Mandell, Liz Marantz, Cindy McKitrick, Anita Morrison, Benjamin Nemerow, Joan Norris, Kathleen Perkins, Virginia Plainfield, Steve Silk, Doug Stewart, Judith Stringer, Maggie Stuckey, Caroline Taylor, Jebra Turner, Martha Wagner, Jisho Warner, Lee Anne White, Karim Winged Heart, Nancy Woods, Heidi Yorkshire and Joseph Anthony, and Gavin Younie.

For my father, Benjamin Nemerow

INTRODUCTION

To see a world in a grain of sand

And a heaven in a wild flower,

Hold infinity in the palm of your hand

And eternity in an hour.

William Blake

Auguries of Innocence

From the beginning the garden has been my refuge, a place where I feel my soul bloom. The first white Christmas rose wakes me out of my winter doldrums and gets my heart beating again. When the feathery pink peonies bloom, I want to eat them with whipping cream. Each year when the Japanese iris unfold, spreading their purple wings etched with white and gold, I stand before them and breathe them in until they are inside me and I have entered their kingdom.

But beyond the beauty of flowers, there's a special kind of garden that's satisfied me most deeply, one that I call a retreat garden. Hindsight shows me that for years I'd seen fleeting glimpses of retreat gardens in many landscapes and was storing the images at the back of my mind. The first time was on a tour of estate gardens in Portland's Dunthorpe district, when I peeked through a yew hedge and spotted an oasis of tranquillity in a neighboring garden. I sneaked in and went directly to what had lured me—a white curved bench at the far end of the garden, with an overhead canopy of lattice, covered with clematis. I sat for a few minutes of perfect peace looking back at the house and garden. There was very little to regard—a few

Whether in a Zen center or a garden retreat, the presence of Buddha evokes a meditative mood. Here he sits surrounded by fronds of sword fern and deer fern with *Primula vialii* in bloom. GARDEN OF STEFANIE VANCURA.

symmetrical beds framed by clipped dwarf boxwood, a green lawn, a stone wall and a low hedge of oakleaf hydrangea. It was tremendously soothing, all that green on green, and the stillness was so relaxing after the hubbub of the tour. I've kept the memory of that garden seat in my mind for ages. Every time I show a slide of it during one of my garden classes people sigh.

Retreat gardens are quiet places that have the power to refresh your spirit and alter your mood, where time has slowed down to the pace of summertime in your childhood, and your senses are as keen as they were then. Only the rustle of tall grasses and occasional clear bird song punctuate the silence. Lilies, honeysuckle and heliotrope radiate color and waft delicious scents of clove, lemon and almonds. Silky poppies and velvety roses sparkling with morning dew invite you to admire their beauty and to reflect on their source. Sheltering hedges and walls divide the garden into small intimate spaces with plenty of places to sit and relax. There is enough time to just be rather than do, to breathe deeply and nourish your soul. Retreat gardens allow us to notice the small miracles of each day: winter cyclamen's bright pink flowers poking through the snow, the spicy scent of cottage pinks, a painted lady hovering above a honey-scented butterfly bush, the Gregorian chant of bumblebees in a lavender hedge.

A place that's used over and over for the same purpose develops its own atmosphere, so that each time you enter it, you are reminded of what you are there for. When visitors enter the Dharma Rain Zen Center in Portland, Oregon, the subdued light, muted colors and spareness of furnishings—black mats and cushions on a gray carpet—combine to form a quiet, calming climate. Offerings on a shrine at the front of the room—fruits and flowers, a sculpture of Buddha and burning incense—set the tone. Years of gatherings in which many have sat together in meditation on these same dark cushions, walked in line together in meditation, and joined hands for dances of universal peace have imbued the hall with a sacred spirit.

Similarly, a space in the garden that's used regularly for reflection begins with visual aspects that encourage peacefulness and reverence. But after being used as a refuge over time, it becomes more than just a physical presence. A garden retreat develops the air of a consecrated place, so that even looking at this part of the garden instills a feeling of ease. And entering that place, we naturally slow down and move into a more reflective state of mind.

In a culture that worships youth it's a relief to notice that the beauty of a fresh bud, an opened flower and a faded blossom are all part of life's natural cycle. In an era that urges productivity and speed, the garden's lessons about pace and timing are a gift. There is no rushing a seed to germinate; eager fingers cannot pry open a bud before its time to unfold; fruit must ripen on its own sweet schedule. The inner clock of plants testifies to a deeper, measured tempo that counteracts our manufactured rush.

So the garden, long a metaphor for paradise and Eden, in fact can offer a climate of eternity to a harried soul. It's a haven where there's time to unravel the complexities of day-to-day life, where the soul has room to breathe. In this quiet, beautiful and fragrant environment, the chaos of the outer world and the commotion in an unsettled mind soon dissipate.

For some, gardening itself—planting and pruning, digging and raking, weeding and deadheading—brings inner peace. Mike Snyder says this about his retreat: "My garden has a relaxed look, but I can't sit—I'm doing, doing, doing all the time. It's my favorite place in the whole world—I love the creating." And Steve Lamphear, in whose garden I felt as though I had arrived home, said this: "Where do I go on vacation? My backyard."

For others, lying in a hammock and appreciating a beautifully designed tableau is the means to serenity. But whether you're a digger or a sitter, you can arrive at the same place—a calm state of mind, where being is more important than accomplishing, where nervous restlessness evaporates.

Some gardens convey this feeling of eternity better than others, and my aim is to show you a sampler of such places and to describe the elements that go into their making. The first chapter helps you find your own unique style by showing you many inspiring possibilities and by suggesting ways for you to get in touch with what speaks most powerfully to your senses, emotions and spirit. The second chapter shows you how to make your retreat private and secluded by enclosing the garden and dividing it into small, intimate spaces. You'll learn how to frame garden rooms

with walls of brick, stone, wood and living plants.

The third chapter addresses the overhead canopy —how to select trees, how to place arbors and pergolas that shade and shelter the retreat. In the fourth chapter I focus on designing the entry garden, which sets the tone and establishes the mood of your retreat.

The fifth chapter shows you how to shape your paths so that they take you through the retreat on a journey that maximizes your pleasure and appeals to all your senses—by hiding and revealing views, by taking you close to fragrant plants, by steering you around bends for delightful surprises. The artful blending of color and texture is discussed in the sixth chapter, which teaches you how to weave flowers and leaves into a rich, unified fabric. The seventh chapter makes suggestions for structures, furnishings and ornamentation—the finishing touches that make your retreat so inviting and welcoming that you will linger there long into the evening. And the eighth chapter shows you how to select the best plants for a continuously unfolding display that celebrates all four seasons.

Of course you will want to make your retreat garden unique, adding personal touches that are your own touchstones for tranquillity. I offer the gardens in this book as inspirations—jumping off places to fire your imagination and get you started. Take the smallest portion, or copy one lock, stock and barrel. There are no patents on gardens. We're all here to learn from one another and from the larger natural world. May your retreat garden bring you the serenity and joy that I've found in mine.

CHAPTER ONE

Finding Your Style

**There is no need
to run outside
for better seeing,
nor to peer from
a window. Rather
abide at the center
of your being.**

Lao-tzu

Creating a garden retreat, like venturing forth on any new project, is a bit of a mystery. How do we start? A few lucky souls have a vision in the middle of the night, but for most of us the process is more like driving in pea-soup fog. You can't see the whole picture, only little glimpses that guide you along the way—the white line at the center of the road, some lights in the distance, an outline of tall trees. This can be daunting, but you must simply go on with your journey, slowly and carefully, but persistently. Fears and doubts arise, but you move along anyhow, even if hunched over the wheel and inching forward like a turtle. Eventually the fog lifts and you pick up speed, but you can't really know that at the onset.

Growing Your Imagination

Your imagination waits patiently for your attention, hidden deep within you in a very safe place. Although the seed of imagination may be small, it has infinite capacity to develop, and it's completely within your power to discover how to make it germinate, grow and flourish.

Ron Wagner constructed this French-inspired curlicue trellis from Virginia creeper branches twined around a rebar support. It frames a view of The Farm, with chicken house, vegetable beds and espaliered apples and pears. GARDEN OF NANI WADDOUPS AND RON WAGNER.

Sometimes the imagination gets buried under the rubble of worry, fear and negativity. Anxious thoughts may cover it up like layers of dry leaves. Self-doubts whispering "I'm not at all creative," clog the imagination like a coat of dry dust. Still, the imagination rests beneath the litter of thoughts like a seed beneath dusty leaves, waiting to be watered.

Creativity calls to us in a very soft voice, like a shy lover. The noise of a radio, car or alarm can easily muffle it. Remember waking up in the morning and sensing the fleeting image of a dream, like a wispy cloud just out of sight? So elusive and tender is creative imagination. Still, it visits every day, waiting for our full awareness. If it could tell us exactly how to find it, I think it would murmur, "Stay quiet, be calm, relax and listen. I am right here by your side, ready to help."

It may be easier to dream up your garden retreat if you let your own dreams guide you from the depths of your very wise unconscious mind. Night dreams and daydreams are gifts from the deep places inside ourselves that help us understand what we long for and what we love, and that point us in the direction we need to go in order to grow.

To get more centered, I do something very ordinary and repetitive like weeding before getting into the more creative aspects of designing a garden. Raking also works wonders. As I pull the rake across the damp lawn and gather red and yellow leaves into piles, all my senses sharpen. I hear the metallic ping of the rake tines, listen to the rustle of leaves, smell the damp air,

drink in the fiery leaf colors. The drone of yesterday's thoughts and worries about tomorrow dissolve into the soothing hum of the sweeping rake. Concerns fall away into the pile of leaves and are carted off with them to the compost pile. As my mind becomes clean and empty, the imagination arrives and begins to paint its beautiful images on a fresh slate.

Weeding accomplishes the same end. As I pull unwanted cress seedlings out of the damp earth around the perennials and dig down with my trowel to unearth dandelions, my concentration on what is right in front of me grows. At first my mind chatters away telling its stories about what happened last night, altering the dialogue to suit my ego, arguing about who was right. But another voice, urging me to remove this thistle and yank out that clump of grass, grows stronger as I continue to weed. Soon the smell of damp earth, the surprising discovery of a slippery newt beneath the leaves, the prickly jab of a rose thorn, take my attention. With each tug, it's as if I'm removing the dross from my mind, weeding the garden and clearing the cluttered brain at the same time.

Once imagination has sprouted you can almost picture it growing somewhere in your mind and your heart, fresh and green as a leaf of lettuce. Like lettuce, it needs to be watered, weeded and mulched. One way to fertilize the imagination is to feed it images

The long stretches of lawn and the leaning trunk of an old apple tree re-create the parks of childhood and bring back the sense of youth's endless time. GARDEN OF BARBARA ASHMUN.

Terry Welch began gardening by growing bonsai when he lived in an apartment, and he keeps them in an honored place near the entry of his current retreat to remind him of the original source of his inspiration. GARDEN OF TERRY WELCH.

of beautiful gardens. The more gardens you visit in person and in books, the more of a repertoire your imagination will have stored away. It's like having a giant box of crayons with all the tints and shades to play with.

Photographing gardens also exercises and stretches your imagination. By framing scenes that please you, you'll learn what makes for a pleasing composition. Sketching or painting a vignette would accomplish the same end—attentive looking combined with replicating it in your own unique way, getting it into your fingers and your eyes so that it becomes part of your cells. No one of these ways is better than the rest or needs to be done to the exclusion of the others. Each one can serve as a way to learn about beauty, to celebrate the infinite variations of composition, to increase your sensitivity to its nuances and ingredients.

Some people contend that shooting lots of photographs interferes with being present and enjoying the garden. But I believe it's just the opposite. If you've ever watched a skilled photographer waiting patiently until the light is just right, framing the composition, studying the possibilities before shooting, it's clear that the process requires even more attention than simply looking. Very much like gardening, photographing a garden with care becomes a communion with the spirit of the place, in which the soul is nourished.

Related arts feed the imagination. Listening to music almost always gives your imagination a chance to breathe. Whether it's Brahms or Billie Holiday doesn't really matter—music is packed with feeling and beauty, just as gardens are. Sweeping away mundane concerns, music transports you back to your heart. It's as if music sings straight to the soul. Poetry too goes right to the heart of things. Metaphors and images bypass the analytical mind and bring us back to what's important. We spend so much time rushing, being busy, avoiding pain. A quiet moment in the presence of eternal beauty, whether through poetry, music or art, restores us to our true selves.

Start with What You Love

Long before landscape architect Terry Welch began developing his majestic retreat that blends a wildlife refuge with a Japanese-style garden, he lived in an apartment where he grew bonsai. "They were my inspiration," he says. "They were my laboratory for experience with plants, and they became my teachers." Like trees, bonsai specimens live longer than we do, if they're cared for. "They're on the brink of death and you have to interact with them to keep them alive. They're like children—you die and they survive you."

When Terry developed his garden, he planned to keep the bonsai there so that he'd never forget the source of his inspiration. As you approach the entry to his home, an amazing collection of bonsai displayed on beautifully crafted benches greet you, still respectfully tended by their owner, who values their effect on his life. Caring for these plants has taught Terry a lot. They instill in him a sense of reverence and admiration. "At the center of everything is to learn to love. Loving them, I learned to love myself."

You can feel this spirit of love everywhere you walk in Terry's retreat. His garden has a pure heart—it reflects the quiet and subtle attention with which he nurtures it. The trees and shrubs gleam with health; even the moss-covered boulders seem to glow with vitality. The stillness and serenity are palpable.

Welch undertook many enormous feats to shape his retreat, but no dream is too big when the labor arises from loving desire. At first the property was an impenetrable thicket of mixed woodland that you couldn't move through without a machete. The ponds were buried, dammed up by the beaver, and Welch had to dredge and remove over a hundred thousand board feet of timber with a crane. Once the ponds were revealed, Terry brought in a moon-viewing pavilion from which to quietly watch beaver and otter glide through the water, and redwing blackbird and cedar waxwing flit through the air. He also built a stone and gravel Zen garden sheltered by a traditional stucco and tile wall.

Yet with all these new developments, he always

Within the vast stretches of a wildlife refuge where nature reigns, this stone and gravel Zen garden reflects man's hand at work, ordering nature's elements into a more restrained picture. This quiet place is perfect for contemplation. GARDEN OF TERRY WELCH.

planned to keep the bonsai and give them a place of honor. It was very important not to forget the source of his inspiration. The bonsai at the entrance to Terry's retreat, in plain view from the patio where you sit and relax, tell the story of where he began.

One step leads to another in making a garden retreat, often in a way that you can't know at the outset. At the beginning Terry didn't know much about the Snoqualmie people who originally lived on this land that was taken away from them. He learned that they were river people who caught salmon and ate salmonberry and that they believed they were derived from the beaver. How interesting then that it was the beaver that dammed up the ponds. After Terry introduced the moon-viewing pavilion he discovered that Snoqualmie means "children of the moon." He was struck by the synchronicity.

Recently Terry developed a new area with a gate opening to a waterfall and pool. "Now the moon gate leading to the waterfall and pool unites Japan with the Snoqualmie people," Terry explains. "The Japanese maple looks across the Pacific Ocean at Snoqualmie

Falls. Both of these peoples had the same common ancestors. Do you see how this garden works?"

The meaning of your garden retreat will grow as you grow, and change as you change. Leave room for the process to unfold and interesting discoveries will be revealed. The love in your heart for particular plants, for a certain shape of rock, for the way the light is cast through the canopy of trees, will guide you to find your way.

Echoes from Childhood

It's no accident that my garden is full of flowers set in beds and borders surrounded by lush expanses of green grass. It resembles the Bronx parks of my childhood where my mother, my younger sister and I sat on a blanket eating sandwiches made with challah and admiring the wildflowers popping up in the lawn. Parks were our only garden retreats from the high-rise apartment buildings where we lived cooped up in small dark rooms. The great green carpets of lawn and the majestic trees fed the hunger of our souls for wilderness, for nature.

Parks were the places where my girlfriends and I wove white clover and small wild daisies into garlands with which we crowned each other. Parks were my private retreats where I escaped to read and daydream, leaning against a favorite maple tree, or lying on my back on the grass watching clouds of camels and sheep drift across the blue sky. So for me, in my garden retreat today, an expanse of lawn and the trunk of an old tree evoke that same sense of luxurious, stretched-out time that resonates from childhood's long, leisurely days.

When I was in my teens we lived near a golf course where enormous weeping willow trees grew, with long branches that swept to the ground like living green curtains. Under these perfectly private shelters I lingered with friends on long summer evenings. The neighborhood I now live in was once a golf course, too, and the big old willows that form the backdrop of my garden retreat are romantic reminders of the sensual summers of adolescence.

When cattails appeared in the small bog in my present garden, a note resounded from the marshes of Flushing, New York, where we lived briefly when I was seven. There my father and sister and I walked on narrow paths dwarfed by velvety brown cattails and wine-colored pokeberry, plants that some consider weeds but that are magical to me.

To this day I picture a lake near the place I grew up where we often went rowing on weekend afternoons. I dipped the oars into the placid water and pulled them through the smooth expanse, enjoying the liquid tug and the gliding motion of the boat. When it was my friend's turn to row I would lean over the side and let my fingers trail through the cool lake and listen to the soft splash of the droplets as they dripped off the oars. I long to have such a lake in my garden retreat to invite the feeling of calmness that I had in that rowboat. All that quiet pleasure will return magnified when I have my lake here and now.

Images from the natural world that we knew in youth carry strong feelings that echo within us years later and make us feel at home. Dream back to your childhood and picture the places that were special to you. Where did you go to relax and just be, to get away and let your mind drift? Where did you spend the long summer days and evenings when you were seven and seventeen? Where did you wander to explore new places, to hike or swim or bike? Picture a few of those places and remember how you felt, what your senses told you. See how you could invite some of those feelings and images into your garden retreat today to bring back the mood.

Re-creating Hawaii

Remembrances of our actual childhood homes and places, magical to us when we were young and strongly tuned in to our senses, are powerful jumping-off places for finding a personal retreat style. For Nani Waddoups, who grew up in Hawaii, tropical plants that grow in wild abandon mean home. When she developed her garden in the Pacific Northwest together with her husband, Ron Wagner, they aimed for a style that would remind them of the lush islands that they both loved. Despite the rainy, temperate climate of Portland, Oregon, they achieved the illusion of a

Shaped like a huge frog, a clay oven sits beneath an all-weather shelter, accompanied by a nearby fire pit, so that the owners can roast, bake and grill outdoors to their hearts' content in any season. The shelter with its peaked metal roof and the bamboo fence have Asian overtones. GARDEN OF NANI WADDOUPS AND RON WAGNER.

Asian touches abound in the hot tub enclosure: an elaborately carved teak screen, bamboo rustling in the breeze, golden Japanese grass (*Hakonechloa macra* 'Aureola') in containers and bonsai pots poised on the stairs. GARDEN OF NANI WADDOUPS AND RON WAGNER.

tropical paradise by choosing plants with big, bold leaves suggesting hotter climates—fig tree, Japanese aralia, empress tree and Japanese angelica tree, to name just a few.

To suggest an overgrown thicket, they chose strong-growing plants with wild, rambling natures—like clematis, wisteria and trumpet vine—to climb and drape over walls and arbors. They thickened borders with tall ornamental grasses and luxuriant ferns, with fast-growing cranesbills and rampant bugleweeds. Instead of growing commonplace cosmos and petunias, they sought out exotic annuals with showy leaves and brilliant, fragrant flowers to emphasize the tropical look—sensational angel trumpet, tall gingers, bold-leaved cannas and chocolate-leaved flaxes, which they overwinter every year in a homemade greenhouse.

Water too plays a big part in this garden and makes it feel more like an island getaway. Ponds, waterfalls and fountains add reflective surfaces and soothing sounds. Large-leaved, water-loving plants such as pickerel, arrowhead and calla lily contribute to the exotic ambience. This garden retreat transports you to another country. Nani and Ron have created their own personal tropical paradise in a temperate climate, which they have named Moot Pointe, by blending childhood memories with the powerful forces of their imagination and capability.

Enter the gate to Moot Pointe and you've stepped into Asia, with fences made of bamboo and reed matting setting the tone. A large stand of bamboo shimmering in the distance and a Japanese snowbell tree confirm your hunch. But the atmosphere grows even more exotic as you approach the house. A large ceramic oven shaped like a frog sits on the patio, which is sheltered by a structure with a painted metal roof. An elaborately carved teak screen beckons you for a closer look, and then you see that it forms one wall of a courtyard containing a hot tub and outdoor shower. Bali, you guess, or Thailand, when you spot the bronze goddess dancing at the edge of the porch. No matter. From the moment you set foot inside, you're on a captivating journey to the East and to whimsy.

"The whole place is an oasis, with a meditative quality," Nani says of her exquisite garden. She and Ron design interiors for stores and restaurants, and they wanted a retreat from the sensory bombardment of a very interactive work life. Books on tropical architecture captured their imagination and they soon built an elevated Thai hut with a steeply pitched roof. From this perch you can view the entire garden—it's an Eastern version of a gazebo, mysterious and romantic.

Originally on a steep bank, the garden is now terraced and divided into a series of intimate garden rooms. A long pergola covered with fragrant wisteria frames the upper lawn; beneath it a bench invites you to sit in the shade and soak in the view below. Lower levels are home to a colorful clematis walk and to a patterned herb garden from which the scents of rosemary and oregano emanate.

Moot Pointe is full of fine craftsmanship and whimsical touches—a mini-farm for growing vegetables and espaliered fruit also contains a chicken house fit for regal fowl. Beauty reigns throughout with details that catch the eye: a series of ceramic pears and apples top each post of the fruit espaliers; an arch leading from one garden space to another has a golden orb suspended from its top; a tin rooster is surrounded by containers of silvery draping annuals; and a sculpture of an enormous pear glows from a shady grove. This garden is a retreat to distant, exotic lands both real and imagined.

Perhaps you too have been struck by a place that felt just right. It doesn't matter if it was a book, a film or an actual country that transported you. Consider the atmosphere and the mood of that destination. What was the landscape like there—was it flat or hilly, forested or open, lush or sparse? What materials were the houses, walls, fences and paths made of? What trees, shrubs, vines and flowers grew there that you could include in your actual garden? Imagine the scents and sounds that would remind you of this place. Consider how you could bring some of its unique

Nestled beneath the canopy of Douglas fir woodland and framed by bamboo, Japanese aralia *(Fatsia japonica)*, purple smoke tree *(Cotinus coggygria* 'Purpurea') and heavenly bamboo *(Nandina domestica)*, The Hut overlooks the entire garden. Furnished for daytime lounging, or nighttime sleeping, this eastern-style gazebo is the ultimate retreat. GARDEN OF NANI WADDOUPS AND RON WAGNER.

A rustic bench invites you to linger for a while in this cozy space surrounded by roses, sweet william *(Dianthus barbatus)* and tall spires of foxglove *(Digitalis purpurea).* Towering plants in a small space re-create the illusion of childhood when everything is bigger than we are. GARDEN OF PENNY VOGEL AND MILLIE KIGGINS.

atmosphere back home with you and make it part of your own garden retreat.

Remember that nothing need be duplicated. Creating a garden retreat gives you a chance to borrow the essence of a place that grabs your imagination and use it as a jumping-off point. Recognizing the feelings that pique your interest will help you find the mood that suits you. When you feel goose bumps or sudden tears or a sigh of pleasure, take note, and let your intuition guide you.

A Personal Fairy Tale Re-created from Childhood

When Penny Vogel was three years old, her parents took her to a garden that belonged to friends, an old couple who loved growing flowers and fruit. There was no lawn; instead there was a path that Penny wandered along, discovering the fruit trees, the flower garden, even the clothesline. The house was like a gingerbread cottage, and around it columbines and sweet william, wallflowers and poppies bloomed in wild drifts like a meadow. Dwarfed by the colorful plants, she felt enveloped in a cozy sense of security.

Later in life Penny and her husband rented a cottage from Millie Kiggins, who encouraged Penny's desire to grow flowers anywhere and everywhere on the large rural property. It became a joint venture, with Millie driving the tractor, building fences and birdhouses, and Penny, an experienced quilter, designing the color schemes and planting and tending the beds and borders. Penny daydreamed about the magical place from her childhood where flowers were sprinkled in a carefree way and used it as inspiration, weaving a similar tapestry to nourish her soul in midlife. Buying perennials in threes and fives and sevens to create ample sweeps of color, she allowed them to self-sow and multiply into carpets.

I didn't know this story when I first visited Penny's garden, but I felt like Alice in Wonderland as I strolled along the paths totally surrounded and dwarfed by billowing flowers. Vast stretches of Shirley poppies and delphiniums and roses and bellflowers embraced me with color and made me feel smaller and younger than my real self. Cottage pinks and sweet william overflowed the edges of the path as if to greet me, wafting delicious spicy scents.

From the exuberance of blooms I could sense the loving relationship between Penny and her flowers. The plants sparkled with health and vitality, growing lush and reflecting the generous care of the gardener who tended them. Just like the old couple whose garden overflowed with flowers and fruit, Penny devoted herself to cultivating a similar garden, and it showed. Many visits later I learned that she'd brought in yards and yards of mushroom compost to feed the plants, and that she did all the watering by hand. Penny drinks her first cup of coffee early each morning while meandering along the garden paths to visit her flowers, checking to see which buds have opened overnight.

This old-fashioned country garden is a retreat for strolling, with many stops along the way. Paths wind amid lavender and lamb's ears, coral bells and cranesbills, inviting you to wander and explore, then

The ultimate summer splendor is creamy pink 'Claire Rose' wedded to vibrant blue delphiniums, each elegant flower spike lovingly staked and tied. GARDEN OF MILLIE KIGGINS AND PENNY VOGEL.

rest and gaze. Benches beneath an arbor draped with purple wisteria invite you to linger and inhale the heady perfume. Look east for a view of snowcapped Mount Hood; look west for the full span of flower borders backed by charming small blue cottages.

A little further, a path edged with lewisias takes you to an arbor draped with rambling roses: magenta 'Russell's Cottage Rose,' peach-colored 'Ghislaine de Feligonde,' and 'Harison's Yellow' usher you through. A whiff of mock orange (Philadelphus) lures you ahead to the chapel dedicated to Millie's parents, where all visitors are asked to sign the guest book. Open the rustic wooden doors and enter the silence; stop for a few minutes of reflection in the quiet room with a stained-glass dove. But not for long—return to the

'Mozart' and 'Red Coat' shrub roses, old-fashioned lady's mantle and sweet william bloom in early summer. In the distance a weathered stable and the canopy of mature fruit trees all spell out country cottage-garden style. GARDEN OF BARBARA ASHMUN.

sunlight to inhale more mock orange perfume and admire the 'Pink Bells' rose, whose flower sprays arch to the ground like a pink curtsy.

In this grandmother's garden from the past, the arbors and benches and chapel remain suitably unpainted—weathered wood fits the old-fashioned style. Split-rail fences and birdhouses perched on wooden posts enhance the cottage garden effect. Late in the afternoon swallows dip and dive, filling the air with graceful motion, and hummingbirds hover above the pokers and honeysuckle like tiny helicopters. Marble the cat nestles into the base of a warm rock, soaking up the summer sun. Everything about this garden says slow down, relax, enjoy the flowers and the view. Here there is plenty of time to stroll, to sit, to gaze, to dream.

Landscapes of the Heart

Hiking with friends, I've found it interesting to notice how each person prefers a particular landscape. One friend was drawn to rocky outcroppings and the fascinating array of low mounded plants that thrive in such stark, craggy settings. For him, crunching about the alpine scree where penstemons bloomed in blazing sun was sheer pleasure. Another friend favored the lush, damp forest trails where ferns and bleeding hearts kept cool company beneath the canopy of immense firs and hemlocks, and the ground underfoot was soft and resilient from decades of fallen needles. For me the peak moment was emerging from the shade into the wide expanses of sunny meadows full of dazzling color—carpets of blue lupine and Jacob's ladder, fiery Indian paintbrush and yellow monkey flower.

When I work with design clients, I notice that the same strong love for particular aspects of nature helps them make choices. One woman completely remodeled her older home at great expense because the view from the east windows looked out on Mount Hood arising in a great expanse of sky. There were many drawbacks to the site. The entry was very steep, with an old, deteriorating rock garden that had to be totally rebuilt with safer stone steps and railings. The backyard was really too small for the family's three young children. Yet they all so loved looking out their dining and living room windows to watch the mountain and the changing skyscape that they elected to stay rather than move. Viewing the panorama of sky, birds, clouds and mountain gave them a feeling of great breadth and a strong connection to the natural world.

As I consulted with them I came to understand. A glance out the window every so often was breathtaking. The vastness of sky, the constantly shifting clouds and the mountain that magically appeared and disappeared depending on the cloud cover were fascinating, soothing, expansive. Sitting in that dining room with piles of garden books and notes in front of us was more like a retreat than a work session. Daily communion with this kind of beauty would certainly alter one's mood and encourage the imagination to grow.

Another client, living in a development where large houses bumped up against each other, longed for flat open green spaces, stretches of lawn and infinite vistas. To satisfy that craving, she often spent weekends at another nearby city where the landscape was open and flat. She plans to move to a similar site in the next few years. Meanwhile, working together, we did everything possible to preserve and emphasize her two small lawns, and to keep the views open from her property to common green spaces beyond, so that she can fully enjoy the borrowed scenery.

What kind of naturescape captures your heart? Do you long for the rushing waters of rock-filled streambeds or placid pools in which sky and clouds are reflected? Do you find solace in the quiet shade beneath big trees, or in the brighter open spaces of flowering meadows? Ask yourself if you'd rather look out from a high elevation, gaze up toward a mountain or be on level ground. Close your eyes for a moment and let your memories take you back to favorite places in nature. What did they look like? What were the scents and sounds of those places? Imagine how you might transplant some of those images and sensations to your present garden retreat.

Sometimes a place that you visit captures your heart and imagination so much that you move there. My friend Karim lived in Oregon for many years, but when he visited Hawaii he felt so much more at home that he transplanted himself there. Later he married a woman who works in Oregon, yet he still lives in Maui for about half the year, for this warm,

A French meadow filled with heavenly blue scillas, made more vibrant by splashes of red tulips, stretches toward the dancing trunks of woodland trees. This pleasing scene can easily serve as a jumping-off place for a vignette in your own garden retreat. LE PARC DE BAGATELLE, BOIS DE BOULOGNE, PARIS.

tropical place where he can garden outdoors and grow fruit and vegetables year round is vital to his well-being.

We can also bring parts of a place we fall in love with back home by recreating the beloved landscape in our garden retreat. When I spent time on the Greek island of Crete, I felt at home in a very deep way. What drew me to Crete in the first place was reading *The Magus* by John Fowles and feeling very intrigued by his mystical descriptions. *The Alexandria Quartet* by Lawrence Durrell, also set in Greece, had captured my imagination years before. When I finally walked along the old village roads overlooking carpets of red poppies blooming on the hillsides, everything felt more familiar than foreign. Maybe it was because everyone was dark-haired and dark-eyed like me, or perhaps it was the luminous light and the low stone walls that surrounded inviting home gardens. An old woman in a black kerchief picking parsley seemed tremendously comforting, like the grandmother I used to wish for. Big-leaved fig trees poised against the stone houses, gnarled olive trees and grapevines on the hillsides felt more like home than the dogwoods and clematis in my own Oregon front yard.

When I returned home I planted red poppies and a fig tree to bring the feeling of Crete into my small city garden. Years later when I made my second garden, I made sure to bring the fig and the poppies with me, and I salvaged the old grapevines I found on the property by building an arbor for them to drape over. I can't grow olive trees in Oregon, but the old

A cut stone basin from India brings back memories of travels to a distant beloved place for garden artist Jeffrey Bale, who has been visiting the Far East for many years. The serene reflective surface of water is captured within and seasonal flowers may be floated as a decorative garnish. Rodgersia's quilted leaves nestle against the basin's rim. GARDEN OF JEFFREY BALE.

Blireiana plum tree with a gnarled trunk that came with the garden has a similar old-country look about it. The gray leaves of *Senecio greyii* and the scent of lavender remind me of the Mediterranean atmosphere that spoke to me on my visit to Crete.

Art As Inspiration

Whenever I work with garden design clients I glance around their homes at the art on their walls and the style of their furniture. The tablecloths, carpets, even the dishes help me understand their taste. I notice if the shapes are abstract and geometric, or more blurred

Robin Hopper's artistic skills as a potter and stage designer are evident in his garden where form and structure reign, and beautiful scenes unfold from every point of view. GARDEN OF ROBIN HOPPER AND JUDI DYELLE.

and impressionistic; if the colors are pale pastels or rich jewel tones; if the patterns are plain and simple or full of elaborate detail. All of these everyday objects with which we surround ourselves reflect what we perceive as beautiful, and these images can guide us in designing our gardens.

Whether we study it consciously or soak it in unconsciously, art in many forms can also teach us how to design a retreat. Even geniuses learn from artists who have gone before them. The great gardener and painter, Claude Monet, is a fine example. When he visited Holland for the first time in 1871, he was very taken with Japanese woodblock prints that emphasized bold shapes and lines, with images of

water, bridges, mountains and trees. This style influenced Monet when he developed his world-renowned water garden, which is strikingly different from the flower gardens at the front of his house.

Of course Monet couldn't help but alter the elements of the original inspiration in a way that expressed his own unique creative spirit. He painted the bridge teal instead of the traditional Japanese red. He constructed a trellis above the bridge railing that echoed the horizontal curve of the bridge and softened the lines of the trellis by adding fragrant white and lavender wisteria. These gracefully weeping branches of willow and wisteria swaying in harmony, along with the heavenly pink water lilies glowing on the surface of the water, make it clear that this is the garden of a French impressionist who is as passionate about color as about form. Even though this part of Monet's garden has many elements of the Japanese-style garden —water as a central theme, borrowed landscape, the use of foot bridges—still, his inner genius personalized it and made it his own.

It was also a work of art that inspired Monet to grow the exotic and bold oriental species lilies, *Lilium auratum*—a painting by John Singer Sargent showing a child surrounded by these immense flowers. Sargent's painting was based on a garden in the Cotswolds. And so we see how a garden inspires a painting, and the painting inspires another garden, the two art forms resonating back and forth endlessly.

The art that you love can guide you to the mood and style of your garden retreat, letting you know what your heart needs for aesthetic pleasure. Let's say that you're very drawn to sculpture. Chances are good that you love shapes, and you might like to emphasize this aspect in your garden retreat by introducing plenty of structural elements—arbors, trellises, benches and well-delineated beds and paths. You might enjoy pruning your trees to expose the shape of their branches, even clipping hedges into green rectangles, or creating some topiary art. Certainly a love of sculpture would at the least point you to architectural plants with crisply delineated forms: layered doublefile viburnum *(Viburnum plicatum tomentosum),* tiered pagoda dogwood *(Cornus alternifolia)* or vase-shaped Japanese maple *(Acer palmatum).* You are also likely to appreciate interesting leaf shapes—rounded hostas, star-shaped maples and bladelike iris.

If your preference is for fabric art, it's likely that texture pleases you as much or even more than color. Seek out plants that possess qualities resembling your favorite fabrics. The silky leaves of *Rubus lineatus,* the felted leaves of woolly mullein *(Verbascum bombyciferum)* and the crepe-papery flowers of oriental poppies *(Papaver orientale)* will delight a lover of texture. Notice how wonderfully smooth a ribbon-bark cherry trunk feels, how much magnolia petals resemble satin. Appreciate the prickly edges of holly, the dangerously jagged cardoon leaves, the leathery foliage of *Bergenia*—each has its own unique beauty.

Visit an art gallery or museum, or browse through some books, to explore your personal preferences in fine art. Are you fond of landscape paintings shimmer-

Shape is an important element in this retreat developed by two interior designers. Well-delineated beds and paths, plants with distinctive form, a graceful urn and a globe-topped column at the end of a long vista all reflect the owners' love of architectural form. GARDEN OF NANI WADDOUPS AND RON WAGNER.

ing with light, or more mysterious Rembrandt-like portraits shrouded in mystery? Do you linger at the more symmetrical and formal styles, and pass by the surrealistic paintings, or is it the other way around? Do your prefer sharply outlined geometric shapes or blurred impressionistic drifts of color?

Even a trip to a boutique, a fabric store or a stationery store will help you explore your taste. Do you reach for silk kimonos or linen jackets? Tailored suits or flowing caftans? Solid colors or detailed patterns? Whatever intrigues and interests you, whatever makes you feel "I love that!" will point you in the direction of finding your own style.

CHAPTER TWO

Sheltering Walls: Enclosure for Privacy and Intimacy

Certain places hold a nearly spiritual importance in your everyday life. A particular restaurant, a booth in a certain bar, the family retreat, a beloved mountain peak.... I call such places "sacred realms." Like harbors, they are realms because they are enclosed places . . . that act as discreet, safe havens in our lives. We can count on them to make us feel secure and content within their walls.

Julie Moir Messervy

The Inward Garden

Before my dream restaurant, Vat and Tonsure, was destroyed by the wrecking ball, it was an unassuming building in the middle of a block next to a funky record store, and only the collection of fine wine bottles in the curbside recycling bin hinted at the retreat within. Inside, plain wooden booths and dark walls illuminated by candlelight suggested medieval times. Classical music and strains of opera drifted through the air. The menu was remarkably constant and centered on simple, good food. You could count on fresh, crusty bread, flavorful wedges of cheese, chunky pâté and robust wines.

But most of all it was the dark booths, each one an island of privacy and peace in the midst of soothing music and soft light, that encouraged the deepest exchange of thoughts and feelings. The enclosed spaces created by the high booth backs fostered intimate conversations and the blossoming of dreams.

It was a similar atmosphere that convinced me to choose my first house out of all the many possibilities. Beyond the kitchen sat a nook with one window that

A sense of enclosure created by tree trunks and an artful trellis, as well as simplicity of design, make this small sitting place a serene haven. The soothing textures of ferns, cyclamen and hellebores and a small circular water feature calm the busy mind into stillness. GARDEN OF DOTTY AND JIM WALTERS.

looked out on the garden and just enough room for a small round table and two chairs. Like the restaurant's booth, the nook was a small magical realm where you felt enclosed and sheltered from the spaciousness of the outside world and the ample rooms of the old-fashioned house. Everyone, including the cats, gravitated to this cozy place to share a cup of tea and conversation. It was just the right size for intimacy and hinted at the comforting climate of childhood, of being held close in sheltering arms.

In the garden we can create the same kind of ambience by dividing large open spaces into smaller, more private enclosures that allow us to relax fully and to breathe in perfect peace. There we close the door to the outside world and experience complete safety. The universe is so immense; scaling down the wide open landscape to proportions that relate more closely to our own sizes makes us feel more at home.

We can do this in many ways, with solid walls that partition the garden into outdoor rooms, or with green hedges that divide spaces. Even partially open structures such as pergolas and arbors, garden arches and panels of trelliswork may be enough to suggest separate compartments within the larger garden.

Solid Walls of Brick, Stone and Stucco

When I first toured English gardens, the roses and perennials made me swoon with delight, but if I could have waved a magic wand and brought home one object from the trip, it would have been one of the old brick walls that remain etched in my memory. One was an ancient ten-foot-tall brick wall that stood between a medieval abbey and the garden of two retired schoolteachers. They took full advantage of its warmth to grow half-hardy shrubs and vines against it. Exotic *Cytisus battandieri* flaunted its yellow blooms against the warm terra-cotta-colored wall, sending the perfume of ripe pineapple into the garden. Platter-sized clematis and rambling roses climbed nearly invisible wires that were strung along the sheltering walls.

The other was the brick wall enclosure around the garden rooms at Sissinghurst, which stir envy in the heart of the most accomplished gardener. Partially covered with ornamental purple grape, and festooned with garlands of small-flowering clematis and fragrant roses, these walls create the illusion of immortality. They say rest within us, we will protect you from all harm, we are here to warm and nurture your plants and to give you sanctuary from the outside world.

Stone walls are similarly protective, offering complete visual privacy, muffling noise and soaking up the sun for the benefit of heat-loving plants. In the northern villages of England where slate is common, stacked stone walls are everywhere, the perfect foil for chartreuse spurges (*Euphorbia characias wulfenii*) and lavender wallflowers (*Erysimum* 'Bowles Mauve'). Stone walls give a brand-new retreat garden an instant

Curved stucco walls shelter this Japanese-style garden from the surrounding natural woodland. The distant tree canopy can be enjoyed as part of the borrowed landscape. GARDEN OF ROBIN HOPPER AND JUDI DYELLE.

feeling of age, durability and permanence. At the same time shades of pewter, charcoal and tan within the diverse kinds of stone—granite, basalt and sandstone, to name just a few—add subtle color variations that are interesting yet easy on the eye. Well-designed walls are really a form of garden art; the gradations of color and the way different sizes and shapes of stones are arranged to fit together like a gigantic jigsaw puzzle are as intriguing to the eye as a piece of sculpture.

The neutrality of stone's earth tones makes selecting plant companions very easy—stone flatters all flower colors, especially the more vibrant tones of magenta, orange and chartreuse. Bright magenta *Geranium psilostemon* or orange *Euphorbia griffithii* 'Fireglow,' which might jangle nerves in a mixed border, can look regal against soothing gray stone.

By comparison, brick, which may be tinted orange or pink, is more susceptible to color clashes. Stick with warm, yellow-based flowers (orange, yellow, lime, red) near orange brick and flowers with cooler blue tones (pink, purple, violet, blue) near pink brick for color compatibility.

Dry stacked walls, lacking mortar, give us the opportunity to tuck planting soil and snippets of sedums, succulents and trailing perennials into the gaps. The tracery of continuously evolving plants draped against motionless stone creates a pleasing polarity of static and dynamic elements for us to contemplate in a garden retreat. Whether dry or mortared, low stone walls that are capped can also double as seating.

Stucco walls too offer complete privacy, warmth and compatibility with just about any color flower and foliage. Sometimes they suggest a Mediterranean style, especially when combined with plants native to those warm, sunny regions. A California garden designed by Bobbi Feyerabend comes to mind. Enclosed by stucco walls, this entry courtyard looks out toward a central fountain surrounded by Spanish-style tiles. Masses of purple sage, Spanish lavender and Santa Barbara daisy *(Erigeron karvinskianus)* billow alongside the steps, while drifts of blue and purple bearded iris rise up alongside them. Blood red 'Altissimo' roses, straight out of *Carmen,* climb the creamy stucco walls. You could just as easily be sitting in a Spanish villa as in a Bay Area garden.

Stucco walls are equally at home in a Japanese-style garden, where companion plants like bamboo and camellia sound an Asian note. At the Japanese Garden in Portland, Oregon, stucco walls frame the lower entry to the garden. The Japanese tiles that cap them and the antique gate from Japan that punctuates the walls leave no doubt about the kind of garden you are about to enter. The Zen sand and stone garden in the interior of the Japanese Garden is also enclosed by stucco walls capped by Japanese tiles.

Wood Walls

When professional landscaper Stephen T. Carruthers designed his own garden, he pictured it in his mind even before he built his home. He visualized an enclosed entry garden to welcome his guests. In Steve's

This Japanese-style courtyard is framed by two house walls and wooden fences. The covered gate welcomes you and at the same time frames the scene. Within, an espaliered pomegranate (*Punica granatum*) blooms against the house wall and a wooden bench at the bend in the path invites you to sit back and admire the details. GARDEN OF STEPHEN T. CARRUTHERS.

words, "I wanted to establish a special personal out-door space that hinted at the hospitable place inside our home." A Japanese-style courtyard appealed to him, and he realized that if he designed his house with two exterior walls forming an **L**-shape, half of the courtyard's frame would be established. The solid house walls would give complete shelter and privacy on two sides, and a simple, nearly solid, five-foot-tall board fence on the remaining two sides would complete the enclosure.

As an art major painting within the limits of a canvas, Steve had learned the advantages of bound-aries. He considers a courtyard very much like a canvas. "The view inside an enclosure is restricted," Steve explains, "but what it's restricted to is very appealing. You get an eyeful from the outside, framed by the gate, and from within, framed by the walls." Although the walls of this entry garden are simple, they are embellished by interesting details. An espaliered pomegranate blooms on one wall of the house, where the shelter and reflected heat encourage ruffled orange flowers to open in summer. Small ceramic sculptures are mounted at eye level near the front door and at the entry fence, one suggesting a sand dollar and another more abstract one open to your imagination. A small pool in one corner is backed by a willowy clump of black bamboo, and grassy-leaved Siberian iris repeat this vertical rhythm at the water's edge. Near the porch the graceful foliage of heavenly bamboo (*Nandina domestica*) and a carefully chosen upright stone remind you again that the garden

is in the Japanese style. A plain wooden bench facing the pool invites you to sit and gaze at the soothing water and the stately bamboo.

In a compact space, especially a fully enclosed one, each beautiful detail is noticeable and important. What you see is close up, and there is no larger landscape to compete with these intimate surroundings. Select each plant and ornament with great care, for each will receive close attention.

Wooden walls transformed Rick Pope and Debbie Gorenstein's corner lot into a private garden where they and their three daughters can retreat from the hectic world of law offices and classrooms. Ideally, the whole lot would be enclosed by tall walls, but county regulations limited the fence height near the corner of the lot so that drivers could see around the bend. Creativity saved the day. At the corner, picket fencing only three and one-half feet tall encloses a soothing green lawn for lounging or playing. Toward the middle of the block, where taller fencing is allowed, a doubly thick five-foot-tall board-and-batten fence screens more fully and muffles the sound of traffic. Behind this buffer a jasmine-covered arbor shades tables and chairs where you may sit in greater quiet and privacy. A wall of lattice framed in wood and covered with

This peaceful courtyard invites wanderers to linger for a few moments and enjoy a serene view of still water. A tranquil picture melds the soft-needled foliage of golden hemlock and the lacy foliage of meadow rue. Foxglove, meadow rue and 'Gay Paree' peonies enliven the picture with flowers in several tones of vibrant pink and cerise. GARDEN OF STEPHEN T. CARRUTHERS.

green vines softly screens this tranquil patio from the lawn just beyond.

Climbers camouflage the extreme differences between styles and heights of fencing. A vigorous anemone clematis *(Clematis montana)* stretches to embrace both the picket and the solid fences, softening the change in level. It drapes and spills over the wooden surfaces, sending a froth of pink spring flowers against the weathered wood.

Every available wall serves as a trellis for growing vines and climbers, offering color for all seasons. Dutch honeysuckle *(Lonicera periclymenum* 'Serotina'), with blue-green leaves and fragrant summer flowers, adorns the house facade. A section of picket fencing is covered with winter jasmine, blooming yellow in the dead of winter. Long canes of 'Don Juan' rose fling themselves up another panel of the taller fence, and double velvety-red flowers bloom along these canes repeatedly in summer, brightening the gray boards. Fragrant lavender wisteria is trained up yet another panel of fencing for a showy spring display.

Penny Vogel and Millie Kiggins live in separate cottages linked together by their collaborative country garden. They decided on the style and heights of their fences as a matter of necessity. "I told my husband I'd been looking at his logging equipment for twenty years and I was sick of it," Penny said. That's when the first six-foot solid board fence was built to screen out the bright yellow machinery and enclose the garden. Weathered to a neutral gray, it makes a fine backdrop for peach and pink shrub roses and fat blue

This formerly plain board fence has been dressed up and heightened with added trellis-work and an attractive top to help screen out newly built tall homes across the street. GARDEN OF NANI WADDOUPS AND RON WAGNER.

Open Walls Allow Glimpses Within

Partially open walls of trellis, wood slats and wood and wire are useful to separate the retreat garden from the outside world, while also allowing glimpses in and out of the space. Their pattern adds year-round structural interest and texture to the garden. Occupying less room than thick hedges or shrub borders, these slimmer partitions are perfect grids for weaving ornamental vines and allowing fragrant flower clusters to drape and spill.

In Liz Lair's garden, tall, elegant redwood trellises screen her retreat from the road. Imagine a child's rendering of the facade of a house with a pitched roof, only instead of a solid wall with windows there's a panel of lattice. Four such freestanding trellises stand side by side to make a partially open wall that admits sunlight and air in winter. In the growing seasons, roses and clematis clothe the latticework, providing nearly complete privacy. All eight posts are embellished with elegant copper-faced caps that emphasize the warm tones of the flowers nearby.

Swinging around the corner from the trellises, shorter, wood-framed panels of wire grid form a fence and an entry gate. The wire grid is so much narrower than trelliswork that it practically disappears into thin air, allowing a full view of the garden within, yet it still gives a sense of separation from the driveway.

I helped design an enclosed entry for friends Donna and Tony Freeman, whose casual cottage-style garden is filled with roses, flowering shrubs and colorful perennials. They decided to make their front yard

delphinium spikes. Millie has topped the posts with her own handcrafted birdhouses, which are well occupied—no matter what season you visit, the air is filled with bird song.

This rambling garden is sited with a breathtaking view of Mount Hood to the east and vast stretches of meadow in the outlying areas. Three-foot-tall picket fences were built to give the garden a sense of separation from neighboring fields, yet still allow an unimpeded view of the mountain.

Eventually split-rail fences were added to frame the garden from the parking area. That way they could provide a welcoming entry and at the same time offer arching shrub roses a friendly shoulder on which to lean and drape. All the wooden walls of this garden are left to weather naturally, in keeping with the rustic setting and the unpainted garden arbors and seats.

A six-foot-tall board fence screens out bright yellow construction equipment and acts as backdrop for roses, bellflowers, foxgloves, poppies and cranesbills. The weathered gray wood suits a cottage-garden retreat and doesn't distract from the colorful flowers. GARDEN OF PENNY VOGEL AND MILLIE KIGGINS.

Split-rail fences are great for partial screening and offer roses enough support to scramble and lean. Millie Kiggins's hand-crafted birdhouse tops the post. GARDEN OF PENNY VOGEL AND MILLIE KIGGINS.

more private after neighbors across the street headed up a number of fir trees; pruning the lower limbs erased what had been an evergreen screen. Since Donna especially loves clematis and climbing roses, I suggested building a structure that could be festooned with deciduous vines. This sunny space is mainly used during the spring, summer and fall, so the lack of leaves in winter is not a problem—it's actually beneficial, increasing the light and airiness in the dark season.

Donna's brother built the sturdy, eight-foot-tall trellis of metal pipe with a grid of concrete reinforcement wire. It's **L**-shaped, forming two sheltering walls that effectively blot out the road. The house facade forms the third wall, and various trees and shrubs leading to the backyard complete the enclosure.

As grapes, rambling roses, wisteria and clematis scrambled up the pipe trellis, the structure all but disappeared under the green foliage and flowers. Donna added annual morning glory vines (*Ipomoea* hybrids) to thicken up the screening during the first couple of years while the permanent plants developed. Leaves of varying sizes and textures make this wall subtly interesting for most of the year.

What was once a public front yard looking out onto the street is now a private retreat where the owners can sit quietly on summer mornings sipping espresso and enjoying the fragrance of wisteria and roses. Their cats prowl the beds and lounge on the small lawn, content in their lush jungle.

Elegant redwood trellises screen this retreat from the road, yet allow air and light to penetrate. Whether clothed by vines during the growing season, or standing alone in winter, they're beautiful to look at. Glimpses of plants on both sides are enjoyed, while a sense of privacy and shelter is maintained. Copper-clad caps topping the posts add panache. GARDEN OF LIZ LAIR.

A woven cedar fence, hand-crafted by Sue Skelly of Poulsbo, Washington, encloses the vegetable beds and separates them from the lawn. Its decorative pattern transforms a useful space into a place of beauty. An old Bartlett pear tree, dotted with the season's new fruit and home to numerous bird houses, has been carefully limbed up to allow inviting glimpses of bronze fennel. GARDEN OF LEE NEFF.

Shrubs Form Sheltering Green Walls

My own privet hedge looks like a green cloud in March as the new buds open and unfurl the year's fresh leaves. By the month's end it will have filled out into a living green wall that helps hide one side of the neighbor's bright white house and concrete driveway.

Although privet isn't my favorite shrub for hedging, I'm grateful that the past owner of my garden planted it well before the neighbor's house was built, anticipating the time when privacy would be needed. Since I'm not a faithful clipper, I confess that the poor hedge looks more like a shaggy beast than a piece of tended sculpture, but it does its job well enough with the occasional haircut, sheltering my garden to the northwest.

In my retreat, informal hedges and casual grooming match the rustic, cottage-garden style. Rugosa roses, species roses and butterfly bushes *(Buddleia davidii)* form a six-foot mixed shrub border that frames the southwest edge of the garden. When you sit on the bench under the old apple tree, this screen is just tall enough to obscure the next yard, yet while strolling, you can still catch picturesque glimpses of the neighbor's horse and stable.

An image of a tapestry hedge that I saw years ago at Hidcote in England lingers in my memory. Purple beech, green and variegated holly, and green and variegated boxwood were carefully clipped into a colorful wall, like an abstract painting. Such a tapestry hedge could be made out of many trees and shrubs that lend themselves to clipping—hornbeam, spiraea, barberry, flowering quince, beautyberry. Graham Stuart Thomas's book *Ornamental Shrubs, Climbers and Bamboos* recommends a smashing combination: flowering quince *(Chaenomeles japonica)* with purple barberry *(Berberis thunbergii atropurpurea)* and plum *(Prunus cistena)*. Imagine the bright coral quince

flowers blooming against those intensely purple leaves. Deciduous hedges are perfectly suited to parts of the retreat that are mainly used in spring, summer and fall. Their coming to life in the spring, and seasonal transformations—displays of flowers, fruit and, in some cases, even fall color—make them dynamic, decorative walls. While screening the outside world, they also act as perfectly beautiful back-of-the-border plants. They may be as utilitarian and plain as boxwood or as flowery and showy as reblooming shrub roses.

Needle Evergreen Walls

In landscape designer Stephen T. Carruthers's garden, every foot of space is precious, and he appreciates the privacy afforded by a narrow hedge of 'Emerald' arborvitae. "What else would give you a tall wall and only occupy two feet of thickness?" Steve asks. He buzz cuts it every four years to keep it at a height proportionate to the size of his enclosure, about eight feet tall. Most needle evergreens may be clipped to the height you desire, taller for total screening, or shorter as backdrop walls over which you may enjoy distant views. In Portland's Japanese Garden, several yew hedges are clipped into medium-height walls to set off the spectacular five-tiered pagoda from sister city Sapporo. Against their dark green needles a purple

A hedge of 'Emerald' arborvitae forms one wall of this sheltered seating space. A dry-stacked stone wall separates the entry from more public space. Wands of foxglove echo the hedge's upward thrust, with violet iris and gray lamb's ears as cool-toned companions. GARDEN OF STEPHEN T. CARRUTHERS.

Arborvitae makes a splendid green backdrop for 'Mary Rose' and 'Erfurt' roses and 'Mrs. N. Thompson' clematis when they are in glorious bloom, and a reliable green wall when the flowering plants are dormant. Instead of placing the shrubs shoulder to shoulder, Margaret de Haas Van Dorsser has chosen to leave spaces between them for a less heavy look, and to allow glimpses of adjacent garden rooms from within this cozy sitting nook. GARDEN OF MARGARET DE HAAS VAN DORSSER AND MARK GREENFIELD.

laceleaf maple makes a glorious display. Over the tops of the yew baffle, a distant view of a dramatic waterfall beckons.

Needle evergreens such as yew, hemlock, juniper and cedar are finely textured and subtle, two good qualities in a retreat garden, where serenity is key. Of all the conifers, arborvitae is probably the most favored hedging shrub for evergreen, year-round privacy. For those who dislike its bronze or khaki tones, 'Emerald' is a better shade of green; still, be aware that it has some yellow tints. If you're sensitive to nuances in color, make sure that the foliage color of a plant appeals to you before installing a whole hedge. So many possibilities await you—from the cooler greens of incense cedar and Canadian hemlock, and the blue-green of columnar juniper ('Stricta,' 'Pyramidalis,' 'Blue Heaven') to the inky dark green of yew.

You might consider how color tones affect your emotions. Do you experience the blue-greens as soothing or chilling? Do you perceive dark greens as refreshing or somber? Do yellow-greens strike you as cheerful or garish? In a garden retreat it's particularly

Tall firs and cedars that form the permanent, evergreen walls of this retreat provide year-round shelter. Pampas grass rises up in spring to form a secondary wall that lasts through summer and fall, separating the lawn with its sitting space from the bridge, pond and house beyond, effectively turning them into enclosed garden rooms during the milder seasons. GARDEN OF NANI WADDOUPS AND RON WAGNER.

important to honor our feelings; our desire to create a tranquil mood asks us to pay careful attention to our personal responses to color, texture and fragrance, and to choose the plants that make us happy.

From a practical point of view, please remember to give yourself a few feet of access in front of any hedge that requires clipping, a little footpath or trail between the hedge and the bed it backs up to—room enough to stand on a ladder, ample space to rake up the prunings. And do ask yourself too if you enjoy clipping well enough to grow a hedge, or if you're willing to hire help to maintain it. Otherwise, an informal border of mixed shrubs may be a better choice and will be equally effective in screening, while requiring just a few more feet of space.

A handcrafted birdhouse is tucked into 'Emerald' arborvitae hedge—the birds will feel as safe and sheltered here as the occupants of the sitting space that 'Emerald' encloses. GARDEN OF STEPHEN T. CARRUTHERS.

Broadleaf Evergreen Walls

A beautiful garden I helped design stands on a very well-traveled road leading to the International Rose Test Garden, but if you drove by, you wouldn't even guess it was there. A twelve-foot-tall hedge of andromeda *(Pieris japonica)* shelters the retreat from the road year-round. In March white clusters of fragrant flowers that look like pearl necklaces drape against the green foliage. From inside the entry garden these shrubs make heavenly green walls against which pink-, white- and blue-flowering perennials bloom in cool elegance. Andromeda is too often grown in front of a window and dug out in its fifth year when it blocks all the light. In the right place, where a wall is needed, it's perfect and can gracefully live into old age.

With so many evergreen shrubs to choose from, lean toward a matte finish rather than glossy leaves. Remember that subtle is more conducive to peace of mind. Stay away from shiny, bright green English laurel and brazen photinia with its bronze-red new growth. In shade or morning sun, consider taller varieties of dark green rhododendron, camellia and andromeda, which make magnificent evergreen walls with a month or more of spring flower color. Brighter green, and beautifully lobed, Mexican orange *(Choisya ternata)* will happily grow in sun or shade, with fragrant white flowers that make a serene addition to a garden retreat. Crush the leaves and you will release the aroma of orange peel.

In full sun try laurestinus *(Viburnum tinus)*, with dark green leaves that recede quietly into the background for most of the year, and pinkish white flowers that look like Queen Anne's lace in late winter and spring. Or choose gray-green *Cotoneaster franchetii*, with arching branches along which modest white flowers bloom in spring and clusters of orange-red berries dangle in fall. Darker green *Cotoneaster lacteus*, also with white flowers followed by red berries, may also be pruned into a hedge.

It takes two gardeners four days to prune the holly hedges that surround the three-acre sanctuary created by the late Jane Platt in Portland, Oregon. But how magnificent those dark green walls are, the perfect foil for pink and white magnolia candles that light up the garden beginning in February. By summer these evergreen walls are nearly hidden by a vast array of spring- and summer-flowering shrubs and perennials that unfurl sequentially, beautifying the borders with texture and color.

This carefully clipped evergreen boxwood hedge forms a waist-high wall that acts as a partition between a patio and a bonsai display area. Low enough so you can enjoy a view of the bonsai over its top, the hedge is still an effective wall that divides space and adds form and structure at the same time. GARDEN OF TERRY WELCH.

CHAPTER THREE

Looking Up: Sky, Trees and Canopy

The dream of my life

Is to lie down by a slow river

And stare at the light in the trees—

To learn something by being nothing

A little while but the rich

Lens of attention.

Mary Oliver

Entering the Kingdom

The year I was nineteen I got to know the sky. I lived in Israel for a year to see if I felt more at home there spiritually than in America, and I enrolled in the Greenberg Institute in Jerusalem. When we crossed the Atlantic on the *Queen Mary*, for the first time in my life I saw the night sky in its full glory, undimmed by city lights. I felt infinitesimal in the face of the vast sparkling display of stars and moon that surrounded us. There was nothing but the dark ocean with its glimmering waves and the enormous canopy of diamonds.

In Jerusalem our dormitory was always full of commotion, but I discovered that on the roof I could immerse myself in quiet to my heart's content. I took my journal there and wrote, and when I'd had enough of that, I'd lie down on the broad balustrade and watch cottony clouds skitter across the blue sky. The warm paving beneath me and the sun baking me from above made me feel deliciously indolent. It was a luxurious return to the senses of childhood.

Our first trip to the desert showed me the night sky in its ultimate glory. Sleeping outdoors in the warm night and watching the sky before slipping into dreams was a nearly psychedelic experience. The

This heavenly canopy hung with temple bells shades a lounging platform screened by 'Barnsley' tree mallow (*Lavatera* 'Barnsley') and plume poppy (*Macleaya cordata*). This haven is only yards away from neighboring houses on an inner city street. GARDEN OF JEFFREY BALE.

heavens were so crowded with stars that they were white even though it was midnight. A sudden flash and a shooting star would streak across the panorama. To a city dweller who grew up in high-rise apartment buildings, this night sky in the Negev was as exotic as the camels in the market square. And to think that it was right there over my head all along, yet invisible to me in New York City. What else was I blinded to in that busy, noisy place?

In my garden retreat today, I prefer the canopy of sky to any overhead structure. What we miss out on early we treasure all the more when we find it. I don't want to miss any more stars or clouds or new moons. I love looking up at geese flying overhead, at the streaks of lavender and orange in the sky at the end of a gardening day. Most of the canopies I've added to my garden are rose- and clematis-covered arbors.

But at the same time that I love looking up, I understand that sometimes a completely open sky can feel too vast, making us seem like insignificant specks by comparison. Sky stretches forever, filled with stars, galaxies and planets fiercely swirling, all wonderful yet overwhelming. In making a garden retreat we may choose to create a universe more in our own image: human-scaled, protected, a place where we can, at least for a while, enjoy the respite of privacy, safety and peace.

Canopy cuts down on the infinity of sky and gives us a sheltering roof over our heads. As babies, we were enclosed by the roof of a carriage that guarded us like a benevolent giant's hand. The overhead shelter of four-poster beds and wedding chupahs connote

intimacy and closeness. In the garden, a well-placed tree offers the same safehold, its canopy a welcome buffer from the blazing sun, the drenching rain, the chilling wind.

The Healing Power of One Tree

A few months after I moved into the small house I now live in, someone set it on fire while I was away overnight. I came home to discover a charred house with yellow crime-scene tape across the front door. At first I thought I was dreaming, but when I knelt down on the lawn to see if the grass was real, it was soft and green and spongy. Like a sleepwalker I found my way to a neighbor's house to make the long chain of necessary phone calls. Although the arson was investigated, no one was ever found guilty of it, and in time I learned to live with not knowing who did this and why. Meanwhile, rebuilding began, and I went to live in an apartment just a few blocks away so that I could be close to my garden.

Beyond the loving support of friends, I could count on three things to comfort and steady me every day: sitting in the evenings in a rocking chair with my boyfriend's black cat Charlie on my lap, listening to him purr while I stroked him and rocked; raking leaves in the garden while the construction workers hammered and sawed; and looking out my apartment window each morning at an ancient oak tree.

I thought about the tree a lot. It had survived scorching summers while the sun beat down on its leaves. It cast shade on passersby and cooled down

A single harlequin glorybower tree (*Clerodendrum trichotomum*) makes a shady umbrella for this garden bench, a canopy much cozier than the towering branches of the natural overstory. Sit here and rest your eyes on a pond edged by moisture-loving yellow loosestrife (*Lysimachia punctata*), variegated sweet flag (*Acorus calamus* 'Variegatus') and variegated water figwort (*Scrophularia aquatica* 'Variegata'). GARDEN OF STEPHEN LAMPHEAR.

the hot apartments. It had weathered many winters, standing strong in the face of rain and snow, ice and wind. I could see jagged stubs where it had lost branches to ice storms and suffered snapped limbs in the wind. But no matter what summer and winter brought, each spring it unfurled leaves as fresh and green as the year before.

My tree couldn't go anywhere to escape its destiny, just as I couldn't run away from my losses. It stood stoically no matter what came along, rooted, grounded and dignified. And so could I. I watched the tree and drew courage from its strong presence, absorbed its strength, flexibility and power to endure.

In the aftermath of that fire, the comforting cushion of home and harmony evaporated, but so did the complications and responsibilities of caring for a home and running a business. For a few months everything was on hold while I dealt with the basics— replacing clothing, furniture, dishes and linens. In a way, that narrow focus was also a gift. It allowed me to pay very close attention to only a few things. It made me appreciate one oak tree that ordinarily I would have passed by as just another tree on the street.

A garden retreat is similar. It becomes a place where each ingredient is important and deserving of our full awareness. It becomes a place where we return

The thick trunks of Douglas fir have been limbed up to admit light to understory shrubs and to afford glimpses of a Japanese-style garden in the distance. The trunk of Amur maple (*Acer tataricum* ssp. *ginnala*) has been pruned open by removing lower branches in order to offer peeks through to adjoining garden rooms. Without selective pruning it would act as a wall instead of the canopy that's desired here to shade the bench. GARDEN OF STEFANIE VANCURA.

friends with it and ourselves in the way that is possible only when there is enough time and quiet to notice what is in front of us.

Ever since I experienced the healing comfort of an oak tree, I have been more conscious of the character and power of trees. Although at one time I was only crazy about flowers, always looking down to admire the perennials and annuals, now I glance up as well to draw on the strength of trees. A tree with outstretched branches often looks like a dancer in repose, arms reaching out to embrace the space below.

We may be fascinated by the infinity of sky, but we also need the security of sheltering canopy. By lowering the ceiling of a space that would normally be open to the vast heavens, trees make a limitless garden feel more like an outdoor room. Just as a roof turns a house into a more human-sized dwelling, trees frame outdoor space into shapes closer to human proportions. Whether you choose one solitary tree, several trees in a group, or a larger number arranged in a grove will depend on the size of your retreat and how much shade you wish to provide.

Planting even one tree is a commitment to the future. Most trees will outlive us. They're a gift to ourselves in our lifetime, and also to the next generations to come. They offer pleasure to every passerby. When I was growing up, a saucer magnolia bloomed across the street in the schoolyard every spring. I wonder how many hundreds of us looking out our apartment windows were thrilled to see the sumptuous pink blossoms open once again.

to paying full attention, not only to the natural world, but also to our inner world. Because it is sheltered and private and limited, we can enjoy it fully and appreciate what it has to offer without being distracted. We can come to know it completely and deeply, and to know ourselves fully and deeply within it, making

Selecting the Right Tree

Every kind of tree has its own unique nature and it is wise to consider those qualities and see if it's suitable for your particular retreat. The size and shape of the tree, as well as the size of the leaves and the branching pattern make for tremendous variations. Beech trees, for example, become huge and grow so densely that the ground beneath them is as completely shaded as a forest floor. Surface roots and impenetrable shade make cultivating other plants beneath them nearly impossible. However, in a big garden there is no tree equal in magnificence. The dark gray trunk, which wrinkles with age, is often compared to elephant hide; the zigzagging branches and elegant, tapered buds make fascinating patterns to watch in winter; and the soft, furred leaves with distinctive pleats are very handsome. Purple-leaved, tricolor, weeping and even cut-leaved forms make beeches very desirable as specimen or shade trees in the right situation—a large garden with plenty of breathing space.

At the other end of the spectrum, more compact trees with daintier leaves are more fitting in a smaller retreat. Even though it is very popular, I never tire of the Japanese snowbell (*Styrax japonicum*). Small oval leaves sit above the branches so that in June the white flowers are clearly seen, dangling like so many hundreds of white bells from the curving, horizontal branches. After the blooms fade, they form small green fruit that remain decorative all summer and fall. Japanese snowbell casts dappled shade, the most welcome sort in a garden retreat, so that patterns of light play upon the plants beneath it. Deep-rooted, it is friendly to an abundance of ground-covering shade-lovers that will grow happily below—Lenten roses (*Helleborus orientalis*), ferns, hostas, astilbes, lungworts (*Pulmonaria* hybrids) and coral bells (*Heuchera* hybrids).

Some trees, like the thornless honey locust (*Gleditisia triacanthos*), leaf out late and drop their leaves early. This is a great advantage where the maximum winter and spring light is desired and there is also a need for light shade during the heat of summer. On the other hand, evergreen trees such as Southern magnolia (*Magnolia grandiflora*) cast shade (as well as leaf litter) year-round. In a retreat where bold foliage is welcome in winter this may be the perfect tree. For a finer texture, a needle evergreen such as Korean fir (*Abies koreana*) may be a better choice.

In some situations a tree that heads up high is what's most desirable. That way you can look past the trunk to enjoy the rest of the garden retreat. Although I wouldn't recommend a sweet gum tree because of its shallow root system that invades nearby beds, I do enjoy many features of the one I've inherited. Its high-branching habit allows an uninterrupted view of the island beds and borders beyond. Squirrels spiral upward on the strong stout trunk, and flickers probe the bark for insects.

Deep-rooted katsura tree (*Cercidiphyllum japonicum*), trained to a single trunk, is a much better choice than sweet gum. A quiet tree with understated beauty, katsura changes subtly through the seasons.

'Osakazuki' Japanese maple (*Acer palmatum* 'Osakazuki') is the most prominent hallmark of this Japanese-style garden. Other important elements present here are the moon bridge, the water and the two bronze cranes now green with patina, poised amid Japanese iris. GARDEN OF ROBIN HOPPER AND JUDI DYELLE.

The leaning, twisted trunk of this old elephant-heart plum tree frames a view of the neighbor's picturesque stable. Roses and purple elderberry (*Sambucus nigra* 'Guincho Purple') bloom, while drifts of 'Husker Red' penstemon, lady's mantle (*Alchemilla mollis*) and bloody cranesbills (*Geranium sanguineum*) romp at their feet. To the right of the plum tree are 'Fall Gold' raspberries, in keeping with the cottage-garden philosophy of mixing ornamentals and edibles. GARDEN OF BARBARA ASHMUN.

Pairs of heart-shaped leaves emerge opposite each other on the branch in a most pleasing symmetry. The new foliage unfurls bronze purple, then pales to light green, deepens to blue-green in summer, and brightens with gold and apricot tints by fall.

In places where you need screening at waist level, choose a tree that branches out at a low point on the trunk. Kousa dogwood (*Cornus kousa*), Japanese maple (*Acer palmatum*), witch hazel (*Hamamelis mollis*), or purple smoke tree (*Cotinus coggygria* 'Royal Purple') are good choices for this situation.

Your site, soil and climate will also help you choose suitable trees for your retreat. The amount of sun and shade available dictate whether your tree must be a sun lover or shade tolerant. It's no use trying to grow *Stewartia pseudocamellia* in blazing sun, for the leaves will burn. The composition of your soil, whether heavy on clay or sand, will also narrow down the enormous choices. Many willows, birches and maples (especially swamp maple, *Acer ginnala*, and red maple, *Acer rubrum*) will adapt well to heavier clay soils, but most magnolias sulk when their feet are wet. Ornamental pears, oaks, madrones, eucalyptus and strawberry tree (*Arbutus unedo*) can withstand drier soils.

Do some research before selecting trees. Your local nursery and county extension service can help you determine which trees grow well in your climate. The suggested reading list at the end of this book will help you locate the best books about trees, as well as mail order catalogs that are full of up-to-date information about new cultivars.

Trees for Every Style and Purpose

When you enter a Japanese garden, whether in Kyoto or Carmel, you will be greeted by certain familiar trees. Black pines (*Pinus thunbergii*), pruned in the cloud style, stand strong year-round. Architectural silhouettes of perfectly shaped laceleaf maples adorn the winter landscape. Flowering cherries (*Prunus serrulata, P. yedoensis*) shimmer with ethereal pink and white blossoms that float in the spring air, then drift to the ground like confetti. The leaves of dogwood and Japanese maples catch fire each fall and illuminate the autumn garden just before the dying of the light.

So if we wish to create a Japanese-style garden retreat, we choose from the above palette and more: umbrella pine *(Sciadopitys verticillata)*, higan weeping cherry *(Prunus subhirtella* 'Pendula'), Japanese cedar *(Cryptomeria japonica)*, hinoki cypress *(Chamaecyparis obtusa)* and katsura tree are all good candidates. Careful pruning to reveal the branching structure and to allow glimpses through the trees to a view of the larger garden beyond them would also be in keeping with a Japanese-style garden.

A retreat in the cottage-garden style calls for a more flowery repertoire. Apple, plum or pear trees would fit the original purpose of a cottage garden, to provide sustenance, while also offering a burst of spring color. The leaning trunk of an old apple tree is also pleasing to look at. The long tassels of 'Purple Robe' flowering locust tree and golden chain tree, and the froth of crab apple and dogwood appeal to cottage gardeners who love color. Since flowers are the main event in this style of garden, select small trees to save room for perennials and flowering shrubs, and choose deeply rooted trees that won't clog up the beds with surface roots.

If you're planning a Mediterranean-style garden, the gray leaves of a weeping silver pear *(Pyrus salicifolia* 'Pendula') will suggest that mood. Bold-leaved fig trees and olive trees immediately evoke the warm Mediterranean climate and are perfect if your growing conditions are compatible. The names alone of Cedar of Lebanon and Spanish broom *(Spartium junceum)* suggest the original places that a Mediterranean garden

aims to re-create. If your climate allows, choose from the many beautiful eucalyptus trees with luminous blue-green foliage.

Besides providing canopy, many trees make wonderful curtains that serve as green backdrops. In my own garden, neighboring weeping willows on adjacent properties are like a gigantic green background canvas against which colorful perennials and roses stand out. As "borrowed scenery," they give the illusion of being part of my retreat, especially from a distance, when the fences and roads disappear from view and the willows look as if they're on my property.

Weeping trees are especially good for backdrops since their branches droop gracefully to ground level, effectively turning them into green walls. Weeping cherries that burst into pastel pink cascades every spring and weeping Japanese snowbell tree *(Styrax japonicus* 'Carillon') have the added charm of seasonal flowers. For foliage value, consider weeping beech and birch, weeping blue Atlas cedar, deodar cedar and weeping katsura tree *(Cercidiphyllum japonicum* 'Pendula').

Some trees are so structurally intriguing that they invite contemplation, just like a beautiful piece of sculpture. Within a garden retreat trees of this nature deserve a special place of their own, where their presence can be fully appreciated. Let them act as focal points and select companion plants that are more subtle and low key.

Variegated Japanese angelica tree *(Aralia elata* 'Variegata') is one such unique tree. It first drew my

A stately snow gum tree (*Eucalyptus pauciflora* ssp. *niphophila*), with ornamental bark and elegant blue-green leaves, suggests a Mediterranean garden. Its gray trunk relates well to the arbors, which frame a seating area overlooking water. The arbor with upturned ends was modeled after a Shinto spirit gate, reflecting memories of this gardener's childhood. 'Tricolor' New Zealand flax (*Phormium tenax* 'Tricolor'), 'Emerald Gaiety' euonymus and variegated water figwort (*Scrophularia aquatica* 'Variegata') add cooling touches to this refreshing scene. GARDEN OF STEPHEN LAMPHEAR.

spellbound admiration at Holehird Gardens in England, glowing at the end of a vista. The branches are horizontal and layered, with green pinnate leaves outlined in eggshell white. The impression is of luminous, shimmering tiers. Although it looks tropical and exotic, it is perfectly hardy to -20°F. In summer, flowers like baby's breath crown the top of the tree, and in fall, pink tints in the blooms and the leaf margins make the tree even more magnetic.

Don't be concerned that variegated Japanese angelica is too gaudy for a retreat garden. It is showy yet also serene. The creamy white leaf margins draw attention to the foliage shape, yet are also curiously soothing. The branching pattern and foliage tints are cause to marvel at the wonders of creation. Be sure to choose quieter companion plants in muted tones of green. In shade, ferns, hellebores and masterwort (*Astrantia major*) are ideal. Where it is sunnier consider white cranesbills (*Geranium sanguineum* 'Album') to emphasize the variegation, or pink kaffir lily (*Schizostylis* 'Viscountess Byng') to echo the pink autumn tints.

Several contorted trees are good choices for architectural focal points in a garden retreat. Zigzagging branches that cascade to the ground in layers are particularly compelling in winter when structure is completely visible. Contorted mulberry (*Morus alba* 'Unryu') is a fast-growing small tree that later clothes itself with large, round, bright green leaves. The craggy, twisted branches of contorted filbert (*Corylus avellana* 'Contorta') are intriguing when bare and come to life in late winter when long yellow catkins, like golden chains, shimmer in the winter sun. Later, the large pleated leaves all but camouflage the tree's bones.

Camperdown elm (*Ulmus glabra* 'Camperdownii') is the ultimate in contorted drama. Wide-spreading, jagged winter branches sweep to the ground like enormous claws. It seems the perfect tree for medieval castles set in mysterious forests. In summer, dark green

A grove of Jacquemont birches *(Betula jacquemontii)* stands beside the pond in winter, white trunks and branches gleaming. Architectural boulders covered with chartreuse moss soft as velvet make a strong counterpoint to the vertical trunks. Birches can tolerate the pond's damp banks, but need the protection of these wire grids from gnawing creatures that inhabit this wildlife refuge. GARDEN OF TERRY WELCH.

leaves that feel like sandpaper cover the branches and turn the tree into a cool hiding place. Whenever I see the green canopy of a Camperdown elm I picture children underneath having secret tea parties.

At Terry Welch's woodland retreat, several trees stand near the lake in small groves. Their beauty reflected in the still water is breathtaking. Placed close enough for their branches to weave together lightly like linking arms, they convey strength and camaraderie. Jacquemont birches *(Betula jacquemontii)* make up one family, their creamy white trunks pure and pristine in the winter sun. I couldn't resist peeling a small curl of papery skin off the trunk as a memento—touching it at my desk brings that quiet winter day back, and in my mind's eye I see the heavenly white trunks shining again.

Dawn redwoods *(Metasequoia glyptostroboides)* make up another colony. Their rough-textured bark and the shapes of the tall trunks, wide at the base and tapering upward, are intriguing. Deciduous conifers, they leaf out with fresh green needles each year, reminding us of renewal. Dawn redwoods are best known for their longevity in the universe; fossil records tell us that they have been present for at least fifty million years. Large trees, growing to one hundred feet, they have a very strong presence. On a big property, these fast-growing trees give a feeling of age to a young garden.

On smaller sites the same delightful effect of a grove may be created with a handful of smaller trees. At Portland's Japanese Garden, three pink-flowering

This vine maple (*Acer circinatum*) allée invites you to enter a corridor that takes you on a circular walk around the lake. In the winter the leafless branches are exposed to display bright green moss, inviting a touch of the soft substance. In summer the canopy forms a shady strolling retreat. GARDEN OF TERRY WELCH.

cherries planted on a hillside shimmer in the spring sun with ineffable grace. Near the teahouse a group of Japanese maples grow companionably and blaze with color every autumn. At the Bishop's Close at Elk's Rock, a group of *Stewartia monodelpha* frame a section of the garden, with cinnamon-colored trunks that warm the winter landscape, camellia-shaped white flowers that open in summer and leaves that turn rich red every fall.

Even shrubs can be used to form groves. At the Berry Botanic Gardens a grove of species rhododendrons (*Rhododendron fargesii, R. decorum, R. calophytum*) forms a magical thicket in the woodland garden. Planted years ago by devoted gardener Rae Selling Berry, who grew them from seed collected by a plant hunting expedition, they matured into oversize shrubs and were sculpted into small trees with judicious pruning. The gnarled trunks and branches lean and twist like wild dancers celebrating the rites of spring. When I first strolled through the woods and came upon this grove, I felt a joyous exuberance bursting from these beings.

This garden arch with built-in benches stands at the south end of a large rectangular grape arbor. Both structures contribute crisp lines in counterpoint to the soft shapes of flowering plants that fill the neighboring beds and borders. 'New Dawn' rose climbs the arch and opens its pastel pink flowers in May, sending a delicate sweet scent into the garden. GARDEN OF BARBARA ASHMUN.

Allées and Arbors

When you want to lead a visitor down a path, flank it with an allée, a colonnade of trees planted on both sides, which turns the passage into a long corridor. Walking through an allée is like receiving a welcoming embrace. The first allée I ever saw was made of lilacs that grew on both sides of a long path, forming an inviting tunnel the length of the side yard. The opulent lavender flowers beckoned and their sweet scent lured me toward the main garden.

Another allée, made of vine maple *(Acer circinatum)*, forms a cool tunnel that leads you on a stroll through Terry Welch's woodland retreat. Snowfall's weight has arched the maple trunks, and Terry has also bent some of the branches to make them curve down and root. The damp climate has encouraged vivid green moss to grow on the trunks and branches so that in winter velvety chartreuse limbs form a colorful corridor; the same allée makes a cool, shady refuge in summer. No matter what the season, this allée is a haven of tranquillity.

Even a small garden can contain an allée of espaliered fruit trees or narrow columnar trees, or even large containers fitted with pyramidal trellises covered with clematis. With a little imagination, anything is possible.

Arbors are also especially welcome in small gardens. Unlike trees that take up moisture and nutrition from neighboring beds, arbors add canopy without depleting the soil. Cooling shade is cast in summer's heat, with the added benefit of seasonally colorful and

In this jam-packed suburban garden, two roses—'Graham Thomas' and 'Apple Blossom'—share the arbor with 'Perle D'Azur' clematis to form a colorful canopy. The single, clustered and double flowers contrast nicely with each other; their colors mingle harmoniously to make a rich tiara. This canopy frames only an enticing glimpse of the border within, as the path takes an artful bend out of sight. GARDEN OF MIKE SNYDER.

fragrant vines that climb the structure. In my own garden, an arbor smothered with 'New Dawn' roses and Hall's honeysuckle wafts scent nearly all summer. Benches built into the arbor provide a little hideaway to sit and cool off, or to have a private conversation with one or two friends even when the garden is crowded with visitors. My cats and visiting cats from nearby gardens lounge here, finding refuge from the heat and neighborhood dogs.

Once built, my arbor and benches begged for a beautiful scene to gaze at, so I followed up by developing beds and borders below. If your scene is already in place, site your arbor where you can best appreciate the view. At Millie Kiggins and Penny Vogel's garden one arbor is placed so that you can look east toward snowcapped Mount Hood or west toward their colorful beds and borders.

An arbor can also act as a picture frame through which you glimpse a perfectly arranged composition. At Wave Hill in Riverdale, New York, a wisteria arbor frames a view of the Hudson River and the rugged New Jersey palisades just across the water. At Portland's Japanese Garden, a wisteria arbor was especially designed to frame a view of a hand-carved granite pagoda, a treasured gift from sister city Sapporo. Concrete posts were installed so that the arbor would have long-lasting strength, but Professor P. Takuma Tono cleverly textured the cement with his hands to look like the bark of nearby Douglas firs.

Pergolas are long arbors or free-standing colonnades that may be constructed in the shape of a rectangle or even built on a curve. In hot climates pergolas provide a shady, cool oasis for strolling or sitting. Benches can be placed beneath them for a refreshing rest between gardening forays. Well-designed pergolas are beautiful to look at as well as beautiful to look from.

For lovers of structure, pergolas offer permanent architectural value, linking home and garden, or home and outlying structures. For the plant collector, pergolas are the perfect vehicle for training and displaying vines and climbers.

Bellevue Botanic Garden's simply built administrative building is enhanced by an **L**-shaped pergola that is home to many ornamental vines. On the sunny side adjacent to the offices a kitchen garden flaunts luscious culinary herbs, and beyond the pergola a mixed border of ornamental shrubs and perennials gives the eye a beautiful picture to rest upon. Benches beneath the pergola invite you to take a break before continuing to explore the further reaches of rockery, woodland and the renowned Bellevue Border.

This multipurpose copper pergola will soon be covered with climbing roses to shade the bench below as well as the path that runs beneath it. An architectural feature within this secret garden enclosed by an arborvitae hedge, the pergola is a beautifully shaped structure to enjoy even in winter when the roses are dormant. GARDEN OF MARGARET DE HAAS VAN DORSSER AND MARK GREENFIELD.

CHAPTER FOUR

The Entry: Portal of Transition

So, a threshold is a savoring place.

Without it, we move unimpeded from

one extreme to another, bumping

up against experiential and spatial

dissonances without cease. With it we

have a point of graceful anticipation

and delight, a spot in which to slow

down and move onward with dignity

rather than with haste.

Julie Moir Messervy

The Inward Garden

Every entry has its unique personality that hints about the space within. When I was little the revolving doors that led into Manhattan's elegant Fifth Avenue department stores were places of great allure. A glass-enclosed, brass-trimmed compartment swept me into the perfumed lobby with an exciting swishing sound, prelude to the luxurious lingerie and magical makeup counters ahead where I would run my fingers through silky slips and spritz perfume on my wrist.

A different kind of magic captivated me at the Bronx Zoo. There I had to pass through a heavy metal turnstile, which slowed me down and clicked me through, stirring up anticipation for the giraffes, seals and elephants on the other side. The sound of the turnstile and its lumbering movement made me even more impatient for the pony rides to come, for the camels with their incredibly long eyelashes. Even these many years later I can feel the wonder and excitement that these passageways stirred up.

It's the same in the garden. Whether you open a mysterious door to a walled courtyard, or unlatch a

The crunch of gravel underfoot, followed by the smooth surface of stone at this entry landing, tells us that we're entering new territory. The bell at the gate reminds us of ancient calls to gather in meditation or prayer. Beautiful evergreen foliage greets us at the landing: *Iris foetidissima, Helleborus foetidus* 'Westerflisk' and a dwarf heavenly bamboo. A glimpse of evergreen golden hemlock beckons from inside the courtyard like a beacon. GARDEN OF STEPHEN T. CARRUTHERS.

garden gate and enter a sheltered grove, crossing a threshold reminds you that you're stepping into new territory. A landing that marks the entry gives you time to pause. This still moment is a chance to take a breath, let go of the outside world with all its cares and open yourself to the presence of a new realm within. It's as if an invisible host were taking your coat and wrapping you in a silk kimono, removing your street shoes and sliding your feet into velvet slippers.

The more senses the entry appeals to, the more evocative and memorable the experience of passing through. The crunch of gravel underfoot followed by the smooth surface of slate at the landing signifies change. A whiff of honeysuckle trained over the entry arch sweetens the approach and suggests that we linger and slow down. An ancient bell evokes images of eastern temples and reminds us of what is eternal. Steps ascending to an entry can also suggest a spiritual journey to a mountain top and prepare us for a more reflective state.

The entry gives us our first glimpse of a retreat, hinting at what lies within. Let the entry set the tone of your garden and establish a mood that invites, intrigues and alters all who pass within its welcoming gates.

The Importance of Evergreens

Since the entry will be used in all four seasons, be generous with evergreens in this space. To make the composition interesting, vary the sizes and colors of the leaves. From the fine needles of hemlock to the broad leaves of evergreen magnolia, there is great diversity in foliage size. Play around with leaf shapes as well—hand-shaped aralia *(Fatsia japonica)*, trifoliate Mexican orange *(Choisya ternata)* and gracefully lobed *Rhododendron daphnoides* are just a few of the many possibilities. Smooth-edged leaves that are simplest emphasize the varied geometry of foliage—oval, deltoid, rhombic, cordate, elliptic and linear.

More elaborate leaf margins provide interesting contrasts. Notice the undulated leaves of the showy purple coral bells such as 'Chocolate Ruffles' and 'Plum Pudding' in comparison to the incised leaves of Corsican hellebore *(Helleborus lividus* 'Corsicus') and the indented pinwheels of *Helleborus foetidus* 'Wester Flisk.' Hollies and some osmanthus have serrated leaves that look like the edge of a grapefruit knife, while the margins of many hardy cranesbills are rounded and lobed.

Then there is texture, or the way leaves feel: crinkled leatherleaf viburnum *(Viburnum rhytidifolium)* and waxy camellia, felted *Senecio greyii* and prickly holly all contribute contrasting textures to the tapestry. It's texture that makes us want to reach over and touch the woolly leaves of lamb's ear *(Stachys lanata),* to stroke the smooth golden leaves of 'Ogon' sweet flag *(Acorus gramineus* 'Ogon'), to run a finger along the edge of a cardoon leaf and see if it's as dangerous as it looks.

Even the way leaves are arranged on the branch contributes to pattern. When they're opposite each other, a pleasing symmetry results. Alternate leaves create a more syncopated rhythm. And there's a certain

Softened by grapevines and anchored by colorful 'Preziosa' hydrangea, this rectangular arch might just as well be a picture frame offering an enticing view of a collector's haven. Glimpses of variegated shrub dogwood (*Cornus alba* 'Elegantissima'), European purple barberry (*Berberis vulgaris* 'Atropurpurea'), silvery *Centaurea cineraria*, and New Zealand toe toe (*Cortaderia richardii*) with its lush plumes, hint at the beauty to be discovered beyond. GARDEN OF STEVEN ANTONOW.

charm that results from leaves whorled around the stem as if they're dancing around a maypole.

For the most relaxing effect, think of blending the leaf sizes from large to medium to small so that the degree of contrast shifts in small increments. Strong contrasts makes the eye jump from one extreme to the other, which is tiring instead of refreshing. A gradual transition without abrupt changes makes for a smoother flow. Let the plants harmonize in small shifts of color as well, for example from dark-leaved yew to medium green camellia to lighter green Mexican orange. Consider the plant shapes and foliage first and the flowers last, for form and texture last many more months than evanescent blossoms.

Seductive Scent

Fragrance is the sense that lasts longest in our memories and draws us in, appealing to our conscious and unconscious minds. Lily-of-the-valley goes to my head like champagne. When it's in bloom, I cut fresh stems frequently so I can inhale its perfume while I write. When a bouquet of white lilacs sits on my desk its sweet perfume brings back season after season of delight, all the way back to childhood when my Aunt Libby's cologne had that same light fragrance. Whenever I smell gardenias I remember how much my mother loved them and the way my father gave them to her every year for their anniversary.

We do our best to put scent into words, saying that purple heliotrope smells like marzipan, but fragrance is best experienced first hand. You have to be

there, inhaling the piercing sweetness of mock orange, the minty freshness of rosemary, the enticing bouquet of chocolate cosmos.

Scent has an awakening effect. In the winter garden a whiff of sweet box *(Sarcococca)* stirs me with a promise of all the fragrances to come when spring arrives. An unexpected sniff of perfume can transform a bleak, cold day into a delightful one, as if the sun has unexpectedly come out from behind gray clouds. In the midst of weeding, a hint of Hall's honeysuckle on the air transports me to a series of endless summers past.

The lovely textures of maidenhair, deer and sword fern, London pride, bleeding heart and dwarf rhododendron contribute ornamental pattern to this shady entry garden. GARDEN OF KEITH GELLER.

bushes *(Buddleia davidii)* perfume the air. Their colorful flowers, purple, lavender, burgundy, blue, pink, white and even yellow-orange last for months, but it's their aroma that casts a spell.

Fragrance dispels worries and soothes the weary mind. If you plant chamomile and Corsican mint underfoot, every passerby releases their healing scents into the air. Let grape hyacinth and sweet woodruff carpet shady places to add their spring perfume to the blend. Tuck oriental lilies between the roses for their luxuriously sweet, clovelike fragrance, and drape spicy cottage pinks at their feet.

Sprinkle flowering tobacco here and there to delight you once evening falls. It's only the species *Nicotiana sylvestris* and old-fashioned tall, white and mauve varieties that have fragrance. Treat dinner guests to a sweet arrival with these pale, star-shaped flowers that are luminous by moonlight and emanate scent only in the dark.

Entries to Spaces within the Retreat

Beyond the main entry, which ushers you in from the street, there are many opportunities within the garden to create further entries. The approach to the side yard is often a good place to frame the view beyond with an arch or an arbor. Especially in hot climates, a pergola covered with vines makes a shady walkway alongside the house and also invites you into the next space by

Scent is especially alluring at the entry, an invitation to explore the beauty within. Train common jasmine *(Jasminum officinale)* over an arch and let the small white flowers scent the air for most of summer. Plant shrubby winter honeysuckle *(Lonicera fragrantissima)* near a doorway where you can appreciate its fragrance on a winter day and mock orange *(Philadelphus)* near the patio to celebrate summer's onset. Once summer has arrived there is no shortage of roses to please the nose—pink 'Gertrude Jekyll' and nearly magenta 'Madame Isaac Pereire' are essential in a retreat. Let honey-scented butterfly

framing it from a distance. Pergolas may unite two structures such as house and garage, or transform a utilitarian but homely garage or carport into a more decorative feature.

After you've passed through a pergola and advanced into further reaches of the garden, its frame offers glimpses back to your starting point. Ideally wherever you stand or sit, a beautiful view is in sight. Arches and arbors, gates and pergolas are frames that allow us to take in enticing hints of the big picture that lies ahead. It's especially important to create vignettes within those frames, or to place the structure so that it frames an already existing vignette.

A garden arch with a few shrubs to either side makes a wall with a passageway through that effectively turns open space into the beginnings of a garden room. It's not necessary to separate garden rooms with solid fences or hedges—you can sketch the suggestion of a wall with a rectangular trellis or a few loosely branching shrubs or even a low-branching tree with multiple trunks. Separating the larger retreat into smaller spaces gives each place a more intimate feeling and creates the opportunity for mystery, surprise and diversity of moods.

At Margaret de Haas van Dorsser and Mark Greenfield's garden, the formal vegetable garden is so well enclosed and framed that arriving and entering is

A woodland trail leads you to this lovely destination: a brick patio with a graceful sculpture poised within a grove of vine maples. Sit at the small table and relax; soak in the peace of this tranquil scene. GARDEN OF KEITH GELLER.

as pleasurable as sitting within and looking out. Four arbors smothered with fragrant climbing roses invite you to pass through, and walls of evergreen arborvitae keep you secluded from the larger garden once you're inside. Organically grown vegetables, bursting with health, flourish within raised beds arranged in a pleasing pattern. Margaret dreamt up the geometric design one sleepless night, in a heartening testimonial to the creative benefits of insomnia.

Keith Geller has transformed his hillside Seattle garden into a private retreat by dividing the space into a series of intimate enclosures. A staircase leading from the street is flanked by pines to the right and a hillside of evergreen shrubs to the left. As you climb the stairs, surrounded by tree trunks and greenery, you leave the street and sidewalk behind, along with the cares of the outside world, and enter a private refuge lush with vegetation. The landing at the top of the stairs welcomes you to pause a moment and notice the borrowed landscape, a verdant hillside in the distance. Open the front gate and enter a brick courtyard framed by false cypresses, a multitrunked vine maple and the house wall. Two Adirondack chairs invite you to sit and relax, at least for a while.

Eventually glimpses of woodland plants beyond the vine maple, or perhaps the fragrance of *Styrax obassia* in early spring, will lure you out of your seat. A narrow path leads you through a miniature woodland where ferns, trillium and meadow rue mingle. Sit quietly for a while on a bench tucked into the shelter of a large shrub and absorb the peaceful beauty around you.

By placing shrubs and perennials on both sides of a garden arbor, you can create the effect of a wall with an open door. In this garden, a clematis-covered arbor, together with its neighboring shrubs, encloses the ornamental garden in the foreground and provides a passageway through to the vegetable garden beyond. Mountain laurel (*Kalmia latifolia*), violet cranesbills (*Geranium ibericum*), white masterwort (*Astrantia major*) and bellflowers (*Campanula persicifolia* 'Alba') combine their blooms in a refreshing color scheme. GARDEN OF STEFANIE VANCURA.

When you're ready to continue, stroll further to the perennial garden that beckons from the next space like a sunny meadow at the edge of a woodland. Savor the colorful flowers and scents and, when you're replete, ascend the stone stairs leading to the larger upper patio. Here the view is open and the space is big enough for a group to gather, with an ample table and chairs.

For more solitude, rest beneath the arbor at the back corner of the garden, where you can look out toward the spaces beyond, protected by a wall and far enough from the main seating area to feel secluded. Just the right size for a private conversation, or for a few moments of reclusive respite, this small getaway is yet another oasis of tranquillity within an urban retreat. The street is only a short distance away, physically, but from within the shelter of your retreat it might as well be in another country.

A Japanese-Style Entry in a Wildlife Refuge

When your home is built on a vast wildlife refuge with ponds and forest inhabited by beaver, otter and heron, how do you signify entrance to the smaller-scale human domain? Terry Welch chose a Japanese-style entry garden to welcome his visitors. A covered gate with a suspended bell, symbolizing enlightenment, greets you as you climb broad stone steps softened by evergreen creepers—crinkly *Rubus calcynoides* and refreshing Corsican mint. Ring the bell with the slender wooden mallet sitting on the shelf above it, and listen to its clear sound resonating in the crisp

In early summer 'Bleu Magenta' rambling rose smothers this arbor that frames a view of the enclosed vegetable garden. Raised beds surrounded by crushed rock paths brim over with organically grown vegetables all summer long. GARDEN OF MARGARET DE HAAS VAN DORSSER AND MARK GREENFIELD.

Stone stairs ascend to this large upper patio sheltered by vine maple and Portuguese laurel where a table and chairs stand for outdoor gathering and dining. On the way up, brush against fragrant rosemary and enjoy the foliage patterns of London pride (*Saxifraga umbrosa*) along the steps, the textures of bold-leaved rodgersia and ferns in the shady back border. To the left is the owner's studio, to the right a smaller sitting nook for complete solitude. GARDEN OF KEITH GELLER.

The final destination in a long stroll through a garden with many intimate spaces is this small nook, beneath an arbor twined with fragrant wisteria. From this place you can look back toward the sunny patio in complete privacy, hidden away behind a curtain of pine and Japanese maple, free to reflect and daydream in the peaceful quiet. GARDEN OF KEITH GELLER.

winter air, with overtones of Japan or perhaps Nepal.

My first view of the garden was on a frigid February day, yet the refreshing textures of pine, cypress, sequoia and spruce buoyed my spirits. Each tree was carefully shaped to delineate its branching structure and emphasize its form, in strong contrast to the surrounding wilderness. Moss-covered boulders, symbolizing mountains, nestled amid rhododendrons and azaleas. One enormous rock with a cavity at its top held rainwater and served as a natural water basin to refresh the visitor.

Two immaculately pruned laceleaf maples guarded the path. The exposed architecture of their trunks and branches made them look like poignant sculptures in bleak midwinter. They seemed to symbolize the strength of plants to weather all seasons, to evoke our own fortitude in harsh times. Beyond the stark maple silhouettes the path took a sharp left turn and continued between a juniper hedge (*Juniperus communis* 'Stricta') and a weathered fence adorned with the branches of an espaliered weeping blue Atlas cedar. The cedar's trunk was thick and white, angled along the fence like a huge elbow; its blue-green needles were of contrasting delicacy. Terry calls it "a dragon coming out to say hello." The columns of juniper and weeping cedar branches along the fence were meant to demonstrate "polarities—the strict geometry of a hedge juxtaposed with the natural flow of blue cedar." Terry prunes the juniper hedge several times a year, even though it's a lot of work, because everyone loves "the blue cigars."

A Japanese-style garden marks the entry to a home built on the site of a wildlife refuge. Pine, rhododendron and Japanese laceleaf maples frame an ascending stone path flanked by moss-covered boulders, symbolizing mountains. GARDEN OF TERRY WELCH.

It's almost as if a friend were taking you by the hand when this narrow corridor guides you toward the sliding entry gate. Blue-green juniper 'cigars' (*Juniperus communis* 'Strictus') form one slender wall of this passageway opposite the weathered fence draped with an espaliered weeping blue Atlas cedar (*Cedrus libani* ssp. *atlantica* 'Pendula'). Slide the gate open to enter the privacy of home. GARDEN OF TERRY WELCH.

This narrow, tunnel-like passage between hedge and fence embraces and guides you toward the house. The controlled flow of space slows you down, shows you how to take in one thing at a time: the juniper hedge and its companion blue Atlas espalier, the weathered fence topped by a tile roof, the wooden gate further ahead with its brass handle in the shape of a fish. The delight of holding the smooth brass handle and sliding the gate open, and hearing the soft shushing sound it made, was not unlike the thrill of passing through the magical revolving doorways of my childhood. I confess that I slid the gate back and forth several times for the sheer pleasure of its smooth gliding motion.

Beyond the gate, the scene ahead unfolds slowly. First the Japanese-style house with its tile roof. Then the entry stream with a stone bridge, below which orange koi flash through the dark water. A little further along a meticulously clipped boxwood hedge frames a section of courtyard devoted to bonsai, forming a low wall that encloses the bonsai benches on one side and a seating area on the other side.

On that winter day the plants were sheltered in the ground, and only the pots, carefully scrubbed and empty, rested upside down atop the benches, waiting to receive their tenants in the spring. In the milder seasons the bonsai, displayed in their beautiful containers, radiate beauty. The diversity of their shapes and the character they display testify to the elegance that comes with age.

Shallow steps lead up from the bonsai benches to a sitting space where two inviting wooden chaises promise warmer times ahead. A round wooden table with four chairs set on a circle of slate hint at summer picnics and soirees. Behind the seats a wooden fence and a group of evergreen arborvitae form a solid wall that completely encloses the space, giving a sense of security. The fences within view of the seats are tall enough to screen vehicles parked outside the gates and shelter this intimate space, yet they are low enough to reveal the borrowed scenery of the native woodland beyond. The boxwood hedge that separates the seating area from the bonsai collection is only about waist high, so although it gives the impression of separating the two spaces, you can still rest your eyes on the beautiful containers beyond.

Everywhere, well-defined shapes please the eye: oval, moss-covered urns, horizontally layered pines, a weeping cherry. A curved path of stepping stones takes you on a stroll through a small woodland, where chartreuse moss and dark green ferns weave a soothing tapestry.

Entering a Tropical Garden

At one time the way in to Moot Pointe was straight down a gravel driveway. The first thing you would see to the right of the driveway was a grassy area with an old sunken cement pond liner, muddy in the winter and barren in the summer. It was called "Otto's yard" because only Otto the dog loved it. But Nani Waddoups and Ron Wagner, indefatigable garden makers, changed that. Both wanted a water feature, and at first they pictured a meadow pond with natural bog plants growing at the edge and a rustic plank bridge.

But events occur in real life that alter the best imagined plans. Their neighbors dug up a driveway and piled the broken concrete right outside Nani and Ron's fence, inspiring Ron to dream up a new scheme, using the concrete to edge the pond and build raised terraces. This helped stabilize the area, which was on a slope that threatened to erode.

Now when you open the gate to the garden, the first thing you see and hear is water. A wooden bridge takes you across a pond surrounded by lush tropical plantings—bamboo that rustles in the breeze, and ginger, with a fragrance that takes you by surprise. A stream of water rushes down an elevated slough and spills into the pond with a hearty splash. As plants grow they will screen the pond from your first approach so that the water will be a surprise, and more shrubs will hide the house from the pond to heighten the element of mystery.

Moot Pointe has many other lovely examples of entry features. The way in to a private courtyard enclosing a hot tub is through an arch in a beautifully carved teak screen from Bali. Two pots of golden Japanese meadow grass (*Hakonechloa macra* 'Aureola') guard the opening like sentries, and glimpses of bamboo within the enclosure invite you to enter.

In the lower terrace of Moot Pointe a rebar arch, softened by vines, frames a view of the herb parterre from the chicken house, fruit espaliers and vegetable garden—known collectively as The Farm. Suspended from the top of the arch, an ornament sparkles in the afternoon light. Even so small an overhead feature can mark your passage from one space to another and prepare you for a surprise ahead, for new images to pay attention to and appreciate. The journey through many territories is made that much more pleasurable and significant by a series of thresholds where one feels on the brink of discovery.

A Quiet Retreat Hidden behind a Holly Hedge

When you park in front of landscape architect Marlene Salon's home, it's hard to see the way in. A tall evergreen holly hedge, interplanted with autumn-flowering sasanqua camellias, shelters this entire corner lot from the road. Eventually you discover a walkway that interrupts the hedge. Several whimsical dwarf hinoki cypresses planted alongside the pavement usher you forward; the pattern of their rippling branches is as texturally interesting as the metal sculptures that emerge like snouts from their centers. Fragrant, winter-flowering witch hazel (*Hamamelis mollis*) underplanted with ferns and bold, glossy bear's breech (*Acanthus mollis*) give a sense of welcome.

When you continue past the front door, a serene enclosed garden unfolds in front of your eyes. A square of green lawn is surrounded on all sides by a subtle green tapestry for all seasons: Japanese camellia, rhododendron, azalea, Heller's dwarf Japanese holly and Oregon grape. In spring, evergreen bishop's hat (*Epimedium x versicolor*) unfurls a veil of delicate

Once a barren hangout for Otto the dog, this area was transformed into an exotic new entryway to a garden that blends tropical, Asian and European influences. Your first taste of the garden is opening the entry gate to the sound of water and crossing this sturdy wooden bridge surrounded by tropical plantings, a complete immersion in sensual delights. GARDEN OF NANI WADDOUPS AND RON WAGNER.

Two archways built of long-lasting rebar and softened by vines invite you to enter and exit The Farm, with its immaculately arranged fruit espaliers and vegetable beds. Each arch frames views of the garden rooms beyond. GARDEN OF NANI WADDOUPS AND RON WAGNER.

yellow flowers and navelwort *(Omphalodes cappadocica)* sends forth a blue mist, both brightening the primarily green composition with drifts of harmonious color.

Several bowl-shaped metal water basins perch in the beds like small lakes, reflecting light and showing the pattern of falling raindrops and petals. Overhead the emerging foliage of three heavenly katsura trees mirrors the heart-shaped leaves of bishop's hat below. The katsuras turn gold and apricot in fall, when the Kousa dogwood and witch hazel color up red. Deciduous trees provide the more dramatic yet fleeting spring and summer changes: kobus magnolia with early white flowers in spring, kousa dogwood with white blooms in early summer.

At one time, years ago, this now secluded front yard sat on a corner lot, fully exposed to the road, with the conventional arrangement of home and garage sitting side by side and a driveway aimed straight for the garage. The garage was converted to a summer house, the driveway was removed, and a new garage was built in a less obtrusive place toward the corner of the lot. The holly hedge was installed to completely enclose the entry garden, and the entire space within was transformed into a peaceful, private retreat. With imagination and perseverance, every front yard has the potential to become a sanctuary like this one.

Even a small feature such as this stone basin brings the soothing element of water into the garden, allowing reflections of light, clouds, raindrops and plant patterns. A stacked stone cairn, used on paths to mark the trail, lends a sculptural presence. GARDEN OF JEFFREY BALE.

CHAPTER FIVE

The Inviting Path

The paths of Islam are straight and narrow,

leading directly into the heart of paradise. . . .

The goose-foot patterns of . . . French

hunting parks tell of the headlong flight

of the stag while English parks may be

patterned on the winding tracks of

the devious fox . . . Japanese gardeners

have deployed precarious stepping

stones with such artful irregularity that

the placement of each geta-contained

foot must become a conscious,

exquisitely shaped act.

Charles W. Moore, William J. Mitchell

and William Turnbull, Jr.

The Poetics of Gardens

Like a thoughtful friend, a path takes you along on a personal guided tour of the retreat garden. It winds enough to hide the big picture, revealing small glimpses that entice you forward. Slowing you down where there's a vista to appreciate, and taking you gently up slopes and down banks in a way that creates interesting views, a well-laid path leads your feet and also instructs your eyes.

A retreat path makes certain that the journey is full of pleasures that appeal to all of your senses. It ushers you through an arbor laden with wisteria so that you linger there to breathe sweet perfume and feel the silky tassels caress your hair. It invites you under a Japanese snowbell tree so that you can look up into the dangling white flowers, it takes you up a staircase to study the nodding winter blooms of hellebores.

A considerate path narrows just in time for your hand to brush against an upright rosemary, the better to pinch its needles and release the minty scent. It takes you single file through a woodland walk so that you are sure to slide your hand along the shiny ribbonbark cherry or peel off a papery length of white birch bark. Just as deep forest shade slowly gives way

In fall the canoe birches (*Betula papyrifera*) glow golden, slowly casting their leaves onto the path that meanders between their white trunks. GARDEN OF MARGARET DE HAAS VAN DORSSER AND MARK GREENFIELD.

When you sit on the red bench in the shade of this long wisteria-covered arbor, you can soak in the long vista that stretches down to the herb garden. The rounded canopies of 'Forest Pansy' redbuds, pyramidal Alberta spruce and colorful clematis frame the path that stretches below. GARDEN OF NANI WADDOUPS AND RON WAGNER.

to dappled woodland before shifting to a clearing's bright sunshine, so the path keeps pace with the changing light and landscape. So subtly that you barely notice, it gently meanders and widens as it escorts you toward the open space of a sunny meadow.

An interesting path occasionally changes its surface to match the setting. A pine-needle trail in the woods shifts to crushed rock near an alpine scree, then becomes a flagstone sidewalk closer to the house. Sometimes the transition is so gradual that there's no need to draw attention to it. But occasionally the path signals that a new territory lies ahead by bending or narrowing. You might like to emphasize a change by flanking the path with two shapely containers that act

as sentries. Transition points are also ideal opportunities for an arbor or pergola to frame the view ahead, separate two distinct garden spaces and usher the visitor into the new area from either direction.

Paths even have unique, delightful sound effects. Expert gardener Steve Antonow paved his primary paths with crushed rock. "I love the crunching sound," he said, "like grape nuts. Gravel sounds more metallic and is more difficult to walk on." Steve also enjoys his secondary paths made of packed earth—he scrapes them with a coal shovel to keep them clean and even. "It's like a meditation, like raking gravel."

Well-placed paths unify a retreat in many ways. From a practical point of view, they connect separate structures and spaces with each other to form a unified whole. Thus the house and garden, the individual beds and the separate structures are all tied together by a framework of trails.

When all paths in a retreat are made of the same material, they serve to unite the garden in the same way that a consistent edging of clipped boxwood pulls together a diversity of beds and borders. For example, a stone path that traverses a woodland, a rock garden and a pond links all three together. A grass path that flows around island beds, and broadens into a larger lawn, unifies the garden with its soothing and uniform green presence.

In a garden retreat relationship is everything. The house and garden relate to each other in size, materials and style; the beds and borders relate to each other in scale; trees relate to understory shrubs and ground

Slabs of cut stone form a straight path across a pond, angling left to allow for more mystery. In a garden retreat, small glimpses of unfolding scenes are more enticing than vistas that show the whole picture all at once. The diversity of stone—large slabs, exposed aggregate, flat irregular stepping-stones and massive boulders—makes a tapestry as interesting as the surrounding plants. GARDEN OF TERRY WELCH.

covers; structures relate to soft-textured plants. And most of all, the paths that run through the entire garden relate to the overall picture: at times separating and defining spaces, at times connecting and unifying discrete elements into a whole, all the while determining the flow and setting the pace.

Paths for Strolling Meditation

Especially in a retreat garden, where a relaxed mood is intended, a thoughtfully designed path teaches us to slow down. By traveling in indirect lines, by taking the scenic route instead of the freeway, a leisurely path sets an unhurried mood. Accustomed to going at breakneck speeds and packing too much into a day, we must be taken firmly by the hand to moderate our pace. A winding path, just like a sinuous country road, seduces us into slowing down and looking around. It teaches us the delicious pleasure of idleness.

Paths are like ribbons that frame beds and borders, sitting places and ponds. The line of the path determines the shapes of garden spaces within its bounds. I prefer curving paths. They meander in broad, gentle sweeps in my own cottage-style garden retreat, suiting the informal, blowsy look. My curved path flows like a river, dividing the spaces into rounded islands of interest—circular, oval and crescent-shaped beds and a half-moon pond.

Paths that run in straight lines carve out square, rectangular and triangular beds within their perimeters, and give the garden a more formal look. A straight path seems too direct a route for a retreat—it gets you to your destination too quickly, without any mystery, revealing everything at a glance. If you prefer straight lines, at least consider angling the path off to the right or left and then continuing forward again, to allow for more surprises. A tree or shrub at the bend will soften the picture and veil the scene around the corner, heightening the stroller's sense of discovery.

Favor the indirect and more evocative journey. Whenever possible, break up long, straight routes to stir the visitor's curiosity. To experience the details of every moment in the retreat garden, we must move slowly and pay attention to the interesting details, whether it's the first Japanese iris unfurling from its tapered bud or the last red leaves of witch hazel drifting to the ground. It's no use to have all this wonder before our eyes if we are whizzing by so fast that it's all a blur.

Primary paths are the main walkways of the garden retreat that take you from the road to the front door, from the back door and patio to beds and borders near the house, and from the front garden to the back garden. Ideally they are at least four feet across, wide enough for two people to walk side by side. These paths, which are frequently traveled in all seasons, should be stable, level and quick to drain and dry off in wet weather. Stone, exposed aggregate and brick are the best materials for main pathways.

Like the main branches of a tree, primary paths are distinctive and contribute to the structural beauty of the garden retreat. In Japanese gardens, the lines and textures of paths are as visually appealing as spring's

The main portion of this beautiful brick path leading to the vegetable garden is wider than its tributary that branches off toward a small lawn and a woodland trail. Gentle curves encourage slow strolling past mixed flowering borders. Durable brick in a sunny site will dry quickly in wet weather, an asset in this Pacific Northwest garden where rain is frequent. GARDEN OF STEFANIE VANCURA.

first flowering cherry. Cut stone, granite, fieldstone and even marble may be used to enhance the pattern.

Secondary paths are like the smaller branches of a tree, still necessary but less pronounced in size and less distinctive in line. Usually they're found in the more outlying parts of the garden that are less frequently visited. They might lead you to the potting shed, through a woodland walk, or to a remote secret garden with a private sitting space.

Secondary paths are often only two feet across, or even the width of a stepping stone, just enough for one person to stroll along comfortably—but never less than a foot wide. For the most part these narrower, more casual walkways are used in milder seasons, the times that we would normally be gardening, so it's not crucial that their surfaces be paved to ensure a smooth, dry surface. Crushed rock, stepping stones, coarse bark chips, pine needles or even packed earth are sufficient for these more casual trails.

When I began my second garden I had two-thirds of an acre and I was so excited about having enough room to plant big borders that I got a bit carried away. One border that separated my house from the road was more than twenty feet deep without any interior footpath for weeding, pruning and mulching. Not only did I have to tread upon my own plants, but every time I wandered through the border I compacted the soil.

Two retired English schoolteachers, in the throes of expanding their garden, showed me the solution to this big-bed dilemma. These experienced gardeners knew how to strategize. They planted two six-foot-wide borders with a two-foot path sandwiched between them, so that from a distance you perceive a fourteen-foot-deep border. Strolling along the inside path you come close enough to enjoy the speckled throats of the foxgloves (*Digitalis purpurea*) and the lacy centers of masterwort (*Astrantia major*). The owners could easily reach in from this same path to tend plants on both sides.

The next year I imitated their technique and built three beds that are eight feet deep, with two separate foot paths between them, each about two feet wide. From a distance this appears to be a twenty-eight-foot-deep border packed with shrub roses, clematis and perennials. The paths in between invite visitors to enjoy the flowers and allow me to garden with pleasure.

Planning the Shape and Pace of Your Path

Nature and necessity are both wonderful teachers. When Bruce Wakefield and Jerry Grossnickle began their garden, they had to make paths first. Their site was a steep hillside with a pond at the bottom, and the soil was treacherously slippery clay. "We needed a way to reach the pond and to travel down the bank to plant trees," Bruce explained. To maneuver a wheel-barrow with plants and compost down the incline, first they had to plan and install paths with decent footing.

"It was easy," Bruce said, "we just followed the deer trails." Often in a rural garden, wild paths are already there to show you the way. At Bruce and Jerry's, the paths undulate gently like hiking trails that switch back and forth along the slope. Especially on a steep site, this method is excellent for tempering the incline. Making paths first also takes care of shaping the beds and borders—the paths become natural frames for the borders that they embrace.

If you don't have the benefit of deer to lead the way, it's easy to lay out the shapes of paths with flexible garden hoses. Leave them in place for a day or two while you study the lines and make sure they please you. If you need inspiration, take a hike in the woods and notice the way trails wind and meander, following a ridge or a creek, moving beneath tree canopy, taking an unexpected turn to reveal a view.

Or take a drive through scenic countryside along an old, secondary road and observe the way it flows.

When you get home, imagine your path as the guide on a tour of your garden and picture how you might like it to lead the visitor through in the most pleasing way. Stroll through the garden alone as if your were taking a dear friend through to show them the garden from different points of view. As you walk, look ahead and glance back to see the scenes that reveal themselves from different places. Notice where a bench might be placed for taking in a picturesque scene. Imagine how a garden arch placed along the path might frame an especially pleasing view.

Try out the tentative path with a companion to see how it works. Does it lead you where you want to go? Does it take enough turns to lend a sense of mystery to your stroll? Does it allow for a sense of delightful surprise and discovery? Is it wide enough for comfort? Make the necessary changes and adjustments so that it goes exactly where you desire.

The materials and the way you arrange them determine how quickly or slowly a stroller will travel through the garden. Where the destination is most important, straight, wide paths made of flat, even paving are best for a quick trip, especially from the

road to the front door. Like a scenic country road, a winding path with many bends and turns will slow the stroller down. Paths made of irregular materials such as cobbles or stepping stones will make for a more careful and slower pace than a smoothly paved sidewalk.

Narrowing the path will also slow down the stride—as will stairs or even a gradual uphill ascent. Interesting details in the path itself will encourage lollygagging—my favorite place to linger is along a pebble mosaic path where I stop to study the intriguing patterns. Plantings along the path that catch your eye, whether flowering ground covers at the edges, a beautiful tree trunk or an ornamental vine scrambling into the canopy, also create interest that slow the pace.

The patterns of brick or stone also determine how quickly you will travel. In his masterful book *Garden Paths*, Gordon Hayward points out that perpendicular brick, laid lengthwise across a path, will make the path appear wider and slow down the foot traffic, while brick laid parallel to the flow of adjacent beds will give the illusion of a longer, narrower path and encourage faster movement.

Stairs, Trails, Steps in an Urban Retreat

Landscape architect Keith Geller's house is perched above a steep bank. "Before" pictures show a staircase shooting straight up the hill like a fireman's ladder. With a vision of a more private, secluded retreat in mind, Geller altered the route, planted with an abundant hand and completely transformed the mood. Before you even get to the stairs, a sumptuous mixed

Secondary paths through more outlying parts of the garden may be narrower and more casual. This slender trail covered with bark winds sinuously, slowly revealing the beauty of the plants ahead, heightening your sense of exploration and discovery. Statuesque bear's breech (*Acanthus mollis*) and lilies rise out of the thick lush foliage of earlier bloomers. GARDEN OF STEPHEN LAMPHEAR.

border greets you at the curb: pink and white rock roses *(Cistus),* purple smoke tree, spurges *(Euphorbia* species) and lady's mantle *(Alchemilla mollis)* offer a warm welcome. The stairs are now divided into two sets of steps, interrupted by a landing about two-thirds of the way up, where you can catch your breath and look around. "Most of the trip is over with by the first landing," Keith explains "so that your hardest work is done and you can relax."

The first part of the ascent may be steep, but the journey is eventful. Birches and pines that screen the road from the house offer a shady green canopy, and thickets of California lilac *(Ceanothus)* and California myrtle *(Myrica californica)* add texture and color. They tell you that you are leaving the public domain and entering a private, secluded garden retreat. As you walk up the staircase you stare into dozens of dark-eyed, chartreuse spurges *(Euphorbia characias wulfenii)* that seem to look right into your eyes. To me, this felt like a soul-to-soul encounter with amazing beings.

At the landing, a detour to the left takes you along a narrow trail through a small woodland. The way the path tapers forces you to slow down and become more observant. Handsome rosettes of London pride *(Saxifraga umbrosa)* carpet the ground, with slender spikes of lacy flowers that shimmer in the dappled light. Fresh green maidenhair fern fronds, sparkling with dew, hover on black stems. Follow the foxglove and huckleberry up to a little seat and savor a quiet moment surrounded by vine maple, sweet box *(Sarcococca ruscifolia), Enkianthus campanulatus* and deer fern.

The narrow path takes you back to the landing, and the second, shorter staircase ascends toward the house. First contemplate the sculptural trunks of two ancient false cypress *(Chamaecyparis lawsoniana* 'Allumii'), the original denizens of the property. A small pond just ahead, with canna lilies beside it, calls for a stop. As you continue along, the path resembles a woodland trail, flanked by fragrant snowbell tree *(Styrax obassia),* dogwood, witch hazel *(Hamamelis mollis)* and Japanese maple *(Acer palmatum).* A carpet of avalanche lilies *(Erythronium* species), ferns, cranesbills, bleeding heart and trillium decorates the ground beneath the trees. A stand of river birch *(Betula nigra)* with shaggy cinnamon-brown trunks pulls you forward toward a brick patio with a small table, three chairs and a special surprise. A beautiful sculpture is nestled into a sheltering grove of vine maple so that it can only be seen from inside the house and within this small garden room.

Steps of stone with pebble and brick in irregular patterns take you up to the next level. The change in elevation and the bumpiness of the stones underfoot slows you down and tells your feet that a change is coming. Geller finds that there is "an intimacy of stone—stone draws you to it. Stone mixed with brick creates an organic flow, smaller rocks to bigger, biggest rocks showing a change of grade, a movement uphill."

The upper brick patio above these stone steps is larger and sunnier, with the feeling of a final destination. An ample table and chairs invite you

As this wide stone path embroidered with woolly thyme narrows down to a wooden footbridge, your pace will naturally slow down, allowing time to glance both ways and enjoy the stream's flow, to take in the yellow flag iris blooming on the bank. Ahead, a broad expanse of lawn encourages you to pick up your pace. GARDEN OF NANI WADDOUPS AND RON WAGNER.

Bumpy steps of stone mixed with pebbles and brick create an organic flow and slow your feet down, preparing you for a change in grade and a change of scene, from a secluded shady sitting space to an open, sunny patio. GARDEN OF KEITH GELLER.

to sit and relax, to look back onto a view of the garden that you've passed through.

A little path off to the right leads to a smaller sitting space beneath an arbor, utterly quiet and comfortable. Ensconced here, listen to the birds or eavesdrop on the murmur of conversation from the larger space that you've just left. Solomon seal and montbretia spears, Japanese and vine maples will keep you safely hidden. Inhale the light sweetness of woodruff beneath the big pine, look up at the purple wisteria on the arbor above and revel in your solitude.

The Embellished Path

At Moot Pointe, Nani Waddoups and Ron Wagner's retreat, paths and steps close to the house are embellished with handmade pebble mosaic. In some places stylized flowers are embedded in the path—white stones at the center, with rays of darker pebbles radiating outward, like so many daisies. Elsewhere a swirling pattern mimics a stream that flows into a whirlpool.

Nani and Ron were inspired by mosaics they saw in Greece and Italy, and also by an instructive *Fine Gardening* article. They sorted river rock into separate colors that would delineate the patterns. Then they prepared and compacted a bed of gravel to serve as a level foundation for the path, and framed it with a wooden edge. They added dry cement mix on top of the gravel, and arranged the pebbles on the surface. When the pattern was just right, they sprayed the finished mosaic gently with a misting hose and allowed

it to set. Sometimes they brush on a clear cement sealer as a finishing touch.

Studying the pebble mosaic slows you down, and makes the garden feel ancient, with overtones of Greek ruins. The subtle gray and black tints of stone blend beautifully with lush green plants and pergolas made of wood. The beds, structures and paths all seem part of an organic whole, where everything is made of natural materials that come from the earth.

Landscape artist Jeffrey Bale's personal retreat is a private oasis that stands in startling contrast to the unadorned urban homes that line an everyday street. Inspired by many trips to India and a deep understanding of garden history, Bale embellished the floor of his backyard with pebble mosaic fit for a maharajah. The lovely chiaroscuro of light and dark pebbles offers just the right amount of detailed pattern in his intimate sitting space, which is centered around a lounging platform covered with richly ornamented Indian fabric. The suggestion of antiquity made by the pebble mosaic fits right in with marble and stone decorative relics from India that are carefully placed within the embrace of tropical-looking foliage and a colorful pink tree mallow (*Lavatera* 'Barnsley').

I watched Jeffrey in the process of making a pebble mosaic Persian carpet for a client's city garden patio. He was squatting on a low bench, surrounded by buckets brimming with stones sorted by color and shape. The ground had been prepared with a bed of compacted crushed rock, and 1" x 4" and 2" x 4" forms were already in place for the long stretch of

patterned border. He mixed the mortar in a wheel-barrow to a fairly soft consistency, then spread it so that it was a little lower than the top of the form.

Wearing protective yellow dishwashing gloves, Jeffrey sketched an **S**-curve with his index finger, then began to lay stones of one color all along the outline of the curve. Deftly selecting rocks the color of charcoal, egg-shell, amber and pomegranate peel, he first squirted each rock carefully with a handy hose-end sprayer—they must be clean and wet in order to stick to the mortar. Then he inserted them, one by one, into the wet mortar and created a complex mosaic in minutes. When the pattern was complete, he placed a smooth board over the whole area and stood on it to press everything firmly into place.

Later on, when the entire stone carpet is com-pleted, Jeffrey will clean the mosaic with muriatic acid to remove any mortar residue, wearing a painting respirator, goggles and rubber gloves to protect himself from liquid acid and rising fumes.

Bale's advice to aspiring mosaic artists: study carpet design in books, in magazine advertisements or at rug merchants, and make sketches of the patterns that appeal to you. Gather the stones so there's memory behind your mosaic, so that you'll remember your time at the river, at the beach, by the mountain. This will lend a more personal, evocative feeling to

Broad stairs of pebble mosaic swirl like a stream and flow into the shape of a whirlpool on the way down to a crushed rock path that travels towards the vegetable garden. In the distance bamboo trellises that support summer's lush tomato vines provide structural interest all year long. GARDEN OF NANI WADDOUPS AND RON WAGNER.

your path and be a springboard for storytelling when your guests linger on a hot summer day.

Just as a path may hold overtones of ancient civi-lizations and personal memories, it can also be filled with symbolic meaning of a mythic nature. To award-winning potter Robin Hopper, whose retreat in Metchosin, British Columbia, just west of Victoria, is a blend of Japanese, English and Canadian West Coast garden styles, the path takes you on a purposeful stroll through the garden. "It tells the story of a journey," Hopper said. "The path is life, and life is like a river that takes you through the woods." We rambled along comfortably in dappled shade, sheltered by the majes-tic canopy of native Douglas firs that Hopper had underplanted with rhododendrons, viburnums and dogwoods. A green tapestry of hellebores, ferns and wildflowers covered the woodland floor.

At first the curving path was embellished by large stones at the edges, just like a riverbed. Then, a series of concrete cast fans made us pause to stop and admire the details. A fan-shaped trellis nearby echoed the forms in the path. "The fan is a symbol of authority and scholarship," Hopper explained. His ceramic studio, Chosin Pottery, demonstrates his expertise as clearly as his artful garden and the books he's written about ceramics, which are studied all over the world. The path meanders toward a large sunny field, symbo-lizing the river meeting the ocean. Hopper will plant a colorful meadow here and place three imposing pillars for vertical contrast amid the billowing wildflowers.

As the path continues, it becomes more of a trail,

winding through less cultivated areas that will eventually become a scree garden and a bog garden. It travels further and arrives at the ultimate retreat, an exquisite Japanese garden that glows like a polished gem. Within, a teahouse pavilion built for meditation overlooks tranquil ponds that reflect sparkling light and pleasing patterns of rushes and waterlilies that are doubled by reflection.

From the shelter of the teahouse you may contemplate a heavenly 'Osakazuki' Japanese maple that reaches fiery perfection in October. The tree's elegant structure is as intriguing as a piece of sculpture. Wooden footbridges that invite you to cross the water link up visually with wooden stairs and a deck that lead to the studio above, so that paths and structures completely blend together.

Hopper has handcrafted an array of enchanting finials in the shape of stylized lotus blossoms to top all the posts along the bridges and footpaths. Near the Emperor's Gate, the traditional entry for the Japanese ruler, cast-in-place stones signal your arrival at a place of complete privacy and serenity. These specially designed details add artful finishing touches in keeping with a ceramic artist's splendid retreat. It's wrenchingly hard to leave this beautiful, peaceful place.

Artful Paths for All Seasons

When Margaret de Haas van Dorsser began planning her garden, she leafed through books until she saw a vignette that spoke to her. A photograph of willow trees with a little creek running through reminded her

Elegant pebble mosaic forms the landing and floor of a small backyard to create an antique Far Eastern ambience. Red, white, charcoal and amber stones were carefully gathered, sorted and arranged by shape and color into swirling patterns. Small crevice plants tucked into the soil form a green tapestry against the decorative stone. GARDEN OF JEFFREY BALE.

of a van Gogh painting. "You see this in Flanders and Holland—black outlines of pollarded trees in a natural setting," she told me. "It reminded me of my childhood, and I thought to myself, I want that!"

Images that evoke strong desire tell you what your heart is longing for. That scene sparked Margaret's imagination so powerfully that she determined to re-create a similar tableau in her own garden. In just a few years she and her husband Mark Greenfield transformed a two-dimensional picture in a book into a living stroll garden that changes with every season.

In place of the creek, a stepping-stone path meanders through a grove of trees. Margaret laid out garden hoses, moving them this way and that until they formed gently undulating curves, just as a creek would. They give a feeling of depth and distance as

The textural combination of stone mixed with pebbles and brick gives your eyes pleasure while signaling your feet to slow down in preparation for a change in grade. Terra-cotta bricks and gray-toned rock blend in much more naturally with green growing plants than a stark white concrete path. GARDEN OF KEITH GELLER.

you stroll along or sit on a viewing bench and look down the path.

She paved the path with flat stones set close together like pieces of a jigsaw puzzle, with just a few inches between them for velvety moss to grow in keeping with the tranquil woodland mood. Spacing the stones close together encourages a leisurely stroll (as opposed to widely spaced stepping stones that invite leaping). The slow pace allows visitors to enjoy the diversity of understory shrubs planted on both sides of the path for year-round color, as well as the low perennials that frame the path.

Canoe birches *(Betula papyrifera)* mark the edges of the path. Their upright trunks create a fine counterpoint to the flat stone path. To vary the vertical

rhythm, clumps with multiple trunks alternate with single specimens. Canoe birches were chosen for their beautiful white bark and for the lacy canopy of small leaves that dapples the light on the path, creating lovely patterns and filtered shade. Seasonal changes add interest—in winter the white trunks gleam, in spring fresh green leaves unfurl, in fall the foliage turns golden. Beneath the birches blooms a tapestry of shade-lovers that provide a long sequence of flowers— pink Lenten roses *(Helleborus orientalis)* and snowdrops *(Galanthus nivalis)* to brighten winter; drifts of crocuses, daffodils and violets for spring; creamy foxgloves *(Digitalis purpurea),* blue bellflowers *(Campanula poscharskyana),* magenta cranesbills *(Geranium sanguineum)* and chartreuse lady's mantle *(Alchemilla mollis)* for summer. The handsome leaves of plantain lilies *(Hosta* species), *Phlomis russeliana* and foam flowers *(Tiarella cordifolia)* enhance and anchor the froth of flowers.

This winding path beneath the airy birch canopy re-creates the beauty that Margaret recognized in van Gogh's painting, and replicates the mood of her European childhood landscape. It has become a central, serene feature in her garden, treasured year-round. Beautiful to view from the windows inside the house, and from a bench poised at one end of the scene, it is equally pleasing to stroll through, a tranquil path for all seasons.

Watercolor artist Chris Keylock Williams had lived in her home for twenty-five years before she created a path that transformed and unified her garden. Existing

After the canoe birches (*Betula papyrifera*) leaf out, the path beneath the trees makes a shady strolling retreat. Peonies, foxglove and lady's mantle bloom in early summer, while the bold leaves of hosta and hellebore anchor the composition. A Colorado blue spruce (*Picea pungens* 'Glauca') glimmers at the end of the path, a cool-toned focal point that beckons the stroller. Flexible hoses were laid out to form gentle curves that flow in the manner of a creek. GARDEN OF MARGARET DE HAAS VAN DORSSER AND MARK GREENFIELD.

concrete sidewalks were serviceable, but as she studied gardens and garden books, she knew they were not suited to her vision of a garden. Williams took about a year to plan a path with character, making many trips to a quarry to select flagstone, granite, large boulders and other stones with just the right shapes and tints. She dismantled an old brick patio that she and her husband had laid in sand many years ago on the same site, and included the recycled bricks in the new paths and patio.

"I loved picking out the rocks and thinking about how to combine round rocks, naturally irregular flagstone and cut flagstones with rectangular bricks," Williams said. When she had her plan clearly in mind

and her materials assembled, she spent two months installing the path with the help of a contractor. "I had to stay ahead of the crew," she said, "laying out the pieces for them to mortar." The transitions from the stone path to a brick patio were challenging, and to accomplish this, Chris wove about twenty large pieces of flagstone into the main brick patio. Then she added a few red bricks to the flagstone path and found several rectangular stones to echo the shapes of the brick.

"I wanted the whole design to be integrated, to come together," she explained, "yet I also wanted something interesting at each turn." To accomplish this, she chose most of the flagstone in tints of gray, tan and pale orange, warm tones that tie together well with the orange brick and red sienna tones of the foundation, porch and house trim. For the love of detail, occasional round rocks and patterns of rectangular gray stones add diversity at bends in the path. Several long, gray stone slabs create a strong center of interest at the entry to the backyard. "Think about entrances and exits," Chris advises. "That's where to make artful transitions by using a new material, by creating a different pattern."

Stone benches that seem to spring out of the garden floor as naturally as rock outcroppings are tucked cozily into curved niches created by the winding path. Sheltering shrubs behind the benches are as protective as the back of a sofa. These seats invite you to plop down for a view of the garden, to watch birds at a feeder or to listen to the soft burble of a trickle fountain that emerges from the head of a shapely tall boulder.

Irregular slices of warm-toned flagstone compose a path that harmonizes with the evergreen rhododendron. A simple stone slab makes a welcome seat along the way and blends right in with the surroundings. GARDEN OF CHRIS KEYLOCK WILLIAMS.

Silver leaves mingled with cool-toned flowers create a serene mood in the garden retreat. *Clematis* x *durandii* weaves its large indigo blooms through the gray leaves of Jerusalem sage (*Phlomis fruticosa*) and also climbs the right corner of the wire trellis. Smaller, bell-shaped clematis chime in—light blue 'Betty Corning' and purple *Clematis* x *eriostemon* 'Hendersonii'—while the larger wine blossoms of 'Warsaw Nike' anchor the left corner of the composition. Pale pink 'Angel Blush' rose campion (*Lychnis coronaria* 'Angel Blush') blends beautifully with silvery-violet alpine sea holly (*Eryngium alpinum* 'Superbum') and 'White Moth' hydrangea. GARDEN OF STEVEN ANTONOW.

front side and warm colors on the back side. The silver leaves support both color schemes and prevent any dissension.

Enjoy the many shades of gray. Some, like lavender and sage, are especially low-key—their leaves are muted, with a matte finish. Woolly mulleins (*Verbascum bombyciferum*) and lamb's ears (*Stachys olympica*) are a brighter gray, closer to white and soft as flannel. Similarly felted, the khaki-gray leaves of

Jerusalem sage (*Phlomis fruticosa*) and the pewter gray foliage of *Senecio greyii* appeal to our sense of touch.

The silver wormwoods—*Artemesia* 'Valerie Finnis,' 'Lambrook Silver' and 'Powys Castle'—seem to radiate light from within. Silver pear tree (*Pyrus salicifolia*) and several shrubby willows (*Salix exigua, S. alba* 'Argentea') shimmer with ethereal light and make retreat gardens glow. Fortunately these glossier gray leaves are also narrow, so their brilliance is refined and moderate, uplifting yet not blinding.

Gray leaves come in all sizes and patterns, from tiny santolina that looks as though it's been woven, to lobed *Geranium renardii* that resembles elephant hide, to the enormous, jagged leaves of cardoon (*Cynara cardunculus*), often mistaken for artichoke foliage. It's hard to overdo gray foliage in a garden retreat. Just remember to intersperse enough green leaves for contrast. I once encountered an all-gray island bed where the plants blended together into a monotonous blur.

Most gray plants are sun lovers that originate in hot regions, and their silvery hues result from a coating of hair or wax that prevents moisture from evaporating. Still, there is plenty of silver for shady places. Lamb's ears happily grow in shade or sun and creeping nettles (*Lamium maculatum* 'Pink Pewter,' *L. m.* 'White Nancy') with nearly white leaves edged in green, thrive in damp shade.

Several fancy-leaved coral bells (*Heuchera*) with foliage that rivals Rex begonias also have silver tints, especially 'Mint Frost' and 'Pewter Veil.' And how to choose between the cornucopia of lungwort

(Pulmonaria) cultivars, so many with gleaming silver leaves? At the edge of a shady bed, 'Spilled Milk,' 'Roy Davidson,' 'Polar Splash' and 'Little Star' glow beneath green shrubs.

For early and late silver accents in shade, be sure to include hardy cyclamen. *Cyclamen coum,* which blooms as early as January with hot pink flowers, earns its keep far past the bloom period with its heart-shaped leaves marbled with silver. And for fall, the pink rockets of *Cyclamen neapolitanum* piercing the fallen leaves are surpassed by the metallic sheen of the patterned leaves. Hardy cyclamen thrive even in the driest shade at the base of big trees.

I love silver leaves at the edge of shady beds to highlight the curved line of the bed as it flows against the green lawn. They're especially effective combined with perennials and shrubs with pastel flowers. My hydrangea dell is a good example: blue, pink and white mopheads and lacecaps bloom there with pink and white astilbes at their feet and an edging of *Pulmonaria* 'Sissinghurst White,' its silver-splashed leaves shimmering in the shade. It looks like a scene the flower fairies would visit.

To taste paradise on earth, take a trip to England and spend some time sitting in the White Garden at Sissinghurst, where Vita Sackville-West combined silver foliage with white and near-white flowers. Delphiniums, lilies, campanulas, balloon flowers, Japanese anemones, foxgloves and tree peonies in pale shades of ivory, blush pink, palest blue and grayish lilac bloom amid silver thistles, lamb's ears, artemesias,

Silver and white are the ultimate in cool, tranquil beauty, perfect to set the mood in a retreat garden. The silvered foliage of 'Silberlocke' Korean fir (*Abies koreana* 'Silberlocke') combined with white Jupiter's beard (*Centranthus ruber* 'Alba') and Santa Barbara daisy (*Erigeron karvinskianus*) makes a radiant picture. GARDEN OF MILLIE KIGGINS AND PENNY VOGEL.

lavender and santolina. Although the White Garden is noted for its monochromatic color scheme, the gray leaves, artfully mingled with green foliage, contribute equally to the soothing, serene ambience.

Sackville-West's plan was to create a "grey, green, white, silver garden which looks so cool on a summer evening." She pictured visitors sitting on a bench and surveying "a low sea of gray clumps of foliage, pierced here and there with tall white flowers." So from the beginning she had intentionally associated the white with gray. Midway between black and white, gray is like a grounding wire for bright white. Especially in the case of large white flowers that arise on naked stems without the benefit of softening foliage, a petticoat of silver leaves is a great benefit. Pure white 'Casa Blanca' lilies on their own are a bit gawky and blinding, but surrounded by a drift of *Artemesia* 'Powys Castle' their elegant flowers relate to the ferny silver foliage and settle right down.

Of the two major focal points at Sissinghurst's White Garden, one is white and the other is silver. *Rosa mulliganii* transforms a wrought iron arbor into a white bower in early summer. An aerial view from the tower gives you an eyeful of the dazzling white canopy. A second silver umbrella sparkles nearby—a weeping pear tree *(Pyrus salicifolia)*. Its small, willow-shaped leaves shimmering in the light add a subtler touch of radiance to the White Garden.

Very much like gray foliage, blue-green and blue-gray leaves have a calming effect on the retreat garden. Closer to green in intensity, they contrast less with companion plants than the glossy silvery grays. If colorful flowers were violins, and gray leaves were violas, then blue-tinted leaves would be the cellos. I find them very appealing, and especially flattering to pink and burgundy flowers.

Blue-tinted leaves are more unusual than gray or green. There are fewer to choose from, but most of them are superb. If you live in a climate warm enough for eucalyptus, many have beautiful evergreen blue-green foliage. The snow gum *(Eucalyptus niphophila)* is hardiest of the lot, to 10°F, and it makes a drought-tolerant, twenty-foot tree with silvery-blue lance-shaped leaves that are attractive throughout the year.

For colder climates, smoke tree *(Cotinus coggygria)*, hardy to -30°F, has similarly rounded blue-green leaves with flower clusters that look like hazy pink smoke in early summer. Both smoke tree and snow gum may be pollarded to keep them shrubby and to encourage the formation of fresh young leaves that are larger, bluer and more rounded.

Katsura *(Cercidiphyllum japonicum)*, a much larger deciduous tree (forty feet and more), has summer foliage with blue-green tints. Like eucalyptus and smoke tree, the blue tints in katsura leaves make it stand out just enough from the surrounding greenery to emphasize its beauty. Katsura's distinctive symmetry —pairs of heart-shaped leaves that unfurl opposite each other all along the branches—makes an eye-catching pattern.

Several perennials with blue-green foliage form refreshing accents in sunny beds and borders. 'Jackman's Blue' rue, grown mainly for its shimmering leaves, is topped by butter-yellow flowers. 'Portuguese Velvet' spurge (*Euphorbia* 'Portuguese Velvet') is also a heavenly shade of blue-green. Bluer yet, the very delicate and flat *Acenae glauca* looks like blue-green lace and thrives in sun or shade.

Blue-green bleeding heart, *Dicentra* 'Langtrees,' with ferny leaves topped by white flowers, has a cooling effect in shade. So does the blue-gray foliage

Amid quiet green Japanese maple and black bamboo, prostrate blue spruce (*Picea pungens* 'Glauca Prostrata') sounds a refreshing note. Color from evergreen foliage such as this spruce lasts all year long, compared to most flowers that color up for a fleeting few weeks. GARDEN OF STEFANIE VANCURA.

of Japanese painted fern (*Athyrium nipponicum* 'Pictum')—its tints are as complex as raku pottery glazes, with hints of pink and maroon.

Blue-green hostas abound for shade. The classic beauty *Hosta sieboldiana* 'Elegans' excels; so does 'Krossa Regal,' a hosta with majestic presence. I love them interspersed with the dainty green filigree of ferns, especially the crested soft shield fern (*Polystichum setiferum* 'Rotundatum cristatum'). They hold court like kings and queens surrounded by their attendants. To keep their leaves unblemished, lure the slugs away with beer.

Warm Tones in Foliage

Wine-colored leaves are dark and have more weight than green. Contrasting with green foliage, they command attention and act as focal points. Sometimes they ground compositions and serve as anchor plants. I find burgundy a rich, satisfying color, thrillingly regal and saturated, but it's not for everyone—some gardeners experience it as somber and heavy. Notice how you feel in the presence of this color. Maroon is a darkened version of red, a red-brown, and marries as well with pink as with peach and coppery colors.

Occasional burgundy accents can be powerful and rejuvenating. Trees with wine-colored leaves are unusual and striking, but since they produce so much maroon because of their large surface area, use them selectively to avoid too much weight. River's purple beech (*Fagus sylvatica* 'Riversii') starts out each year with coppery new foliage that turns deep maroon and holds its color through the summer. The lightly furred and pleated beech leaves are a wonder all on their own; the color changes are all the more captivating.

Purple-leaved 'Forest Pansy' redbud (*Cercis canadensis* 'Forest Pansy') is equally entrancing. Heart-shaped leaves emerge as glossy as if they've been painted with egg white. 'Royal Purple' smoke tree *(Cotinus)* and 'Guincho Purple' elderberry *(Sambucus)* are also excellent. Both have beautifully shaped leaves, the smoke tree's rounded, the elderberry's pinnate, and both may be pollarded in spring to keep them compact. The smoke tree holds its color far longer than the elderberry, which fades to a muted bronze-green by early summer.

Maroon-leaved perennials can keep this rich color going at ground level. It's hard to select just a few fancy-leaved coral bells, but if my hand were forced, I'd pick 'Plum Pudding' and 'Bressingham Bronze' for the delicious shades of wine in their leaves. 'Plum Pudding' glows with burgundy and pink while 'Bressingham Bronze' is a deep dark chocolate maroon. Surround burgundy-leaved perennials with green- or gray-leaved plants. Otherwise their dark leaves blend into the color of the soil and disappear visually.

Golden leaves are like pools of sunshine in the retreat. Especially in shady places these light-reflective warm accents draw attention to themselves. Placing yellow-leaved plants along a path or a vista is a sure way to guide the visitor in that direction.

Marian Raitz, who gardens in Bellevue, Washington, skillfully uses golden foliage to lead you down a hillside path that links the cultivated part of her garden with indigenous woodland. Looking from the top of the slope, you can see golden *Choisya* 'Sundance' sparkling in partial shade halfway down. At the bottom, *Robinia* 'Frisia' glows like a golden beacon amid the more somber, dark green native firs. These two golden-leaved plants light the way down and pull you into the woodland. Luminous *Hypericum* 'Summergold,' 'Sutherland Gold' cutleaf elderberry (*Sambucus racemosa* 'Sutherland Gold') and 'Dart's Gold' ninebark (*Physocarpus opulifolius* 'Dart's Gold') could serve the same purpose.

You might like to light a shady path by edging it with golden Japanese grass (*Hachonekloa macra* 'Aureloa'). The glimmering leaves will show you the way almost as well as luminarias on a dark night.

Use golden-leaved perennials in the retreat garden to brighten dark places and serve as purposeful accents to create a rhythm. Let moderation and proportion guide you. The recent craze for golden-leaved plants can lead to a busy, jumpy garden. A little gold, used tastefully and with some restraint, goes a long way.

The rich wine-colored leaves of purple smoke tree are echoed by the sumptuous purple bearded iris, a smoldering study in deep tones. GARDEN OF MILLIE KIGGINS AND PENNY VOGEL.

The Effect of Variegated Leaves

Green variegated with white translates as pale green or cream depending on how much of the leaf is variegated. 'Morning Light' grass (*Miscanthus sinensis* 'Morning Light') practically glows, since the proportion of white on its slender blades is significant, while 'Francee' hosta, with a narrow white edge on a much broader green leaf, is subtler and comes across as a minted green. I prefer a variegation that traces the edges of leaves—to my eyes this is tidier and more attractive that splashes of white here and there. Notice what appeals to you.

The size and shape of leaves make a big difference too. 'Elegantissima' shrubby dogwood, with medium-sized oval leaves that are tinted cream at the margins, appears to be cool, icy green, while variegated elderberry, with larger compound leaves, makes a much brighter, attention-grabbing impression. One variegated elderberry goes a long way, but you can hardly intersperse too many 'Elegantissima' dogwoods in a retreat. Each one makes a cool, refreshing accent and accommodates as well to sunny spots as to partial shade.

Yellow variegation will create more and brighter light than cream or white. Too many plants of this nature make a retreat very busy and overly energetic. An occasional accent, placed amid similarly warm-toned leaves and flowers (those related to orange, red, yellow or yellow-green), is enlivening. 'Hedgerows Gold' shrub dogwood (*Cornus stolonifera* 'Hedgerows Gold') is a favorite, with golden edges brightening the leaf margins all spring and summer. In fall, pink-red tints warm up the leaves. *Phlomis russeliana* makes a good color echo nearby. Its refreshing oval green leaves carpet the ground year-round and the butter-yellow flowers, stacked in layers, whorl around sturdy stems.

Gradual Transitions Are Best

Becoming aware of all the diverse colors of leaves as well as their varied textures will help you create an interesting retreat. But to foster tranquillity, keep in mind one key principle: orchestrate transitions very gradually, whether of color, size or texture. The result will be a harmonious and unified garden.

The shapely, rich maroon leaves of 'Brunette' bugbane (*Cimicifuga ramosa* 'Brunette') are the perfect foil for cherry red flowers of 'Hadspen Blood' masterwort (*Astrantia major* 'Hadspen Blood'). Both plants appreciate regular watering and shade, especially from the afternoon sun. GARDEN OF ERNIE AND MARIETTA O'BYRNE.

Avoid strong contrasts. In garden design, as in art and fashion, dramatic shifts of color and texture create a stir. For example, the eye is riveted by a golden-leaved mock orange (*Philadelphus coronarius* 'Aureus') set against a black-green yew hedge. This is wonderfully exciting, yet far from the restful and relaxing atmosphere we intend to create in a garden retreat. Small and gradual shifts of color and texture will afford smoothly blended compositions and create a soothing mood.

So if you'd like to place a purple smoke tree (*Cotinus coggygria* 'Royal Purple') within the retreat, don't combine it with a golden elderberry (*Sambucus racemosa* 'Sutherland Gold')—both plants together will create too much commotion. Instead, aim for a more gradual transition, and accompany the smoke tree with a bronze-toned glossy abelia *(Abelia grandiflora)* or, in shade, with a dark green summersweet *(Clethra alnifolia)*. Do likewise with the golden elderberry— combine it with a medium green privet honeysuckle *(Lonicera pileata)* for subtle blending of foliage color.

Texture should be treated similarly. A large-leaved, glossy Japanese aralia *(Fatsia japonica)* beside a dainty-leaved, dark green sweet box *(Sarcococca confusa)* produces too much contrast and jars us. Instead, combine the aralia with a Mexican orange—both are shades of yellow-green, and the Mexican orange

An artful balance between green foliage and occasional accents of gold brighten the shade. Golden fullmoon maple (*Acer japonicum* 'Aureum'), golden cutleaf elderberry (*Sambucus racemosa* 'Plumosa Aurea'), variegated hostas and sweet flags add light, while a purple Japanese laceleaf maple anchors the composition with its dark leaves. GARDEN OF STEFANIE VANCURA.

has medium-sized leaves that make a more gradual transition from the aralia's bold ones. The dark, fine-leaved sweet box is better paired with plants that have moderate-sized leaves in medium to dark shades of green—mountain laurel *(Kalmia latifolia)* or *Rhododendron daphnoides.*

Flowers: Prima Donnas and a Supporting Cast

Flowers vary a great deal in color, size, texture, shape and length of bloom period. Some blend very easily with their neighbors—their color mixes well with most others and their size is modest rather than huge. For example, many blue and blue-violet flowers such as love-in-a-mist, bellflowers *(Campanula),* gentians and cranesbills *(Geranium)* complement a wide range of companions. Creamy-white, pastel pink, pale yellow and light lavender flowers mix well too. I call these sociable, easy-blending flowers that pair up well with most other plants, the supporting cast.

Golden Japanese grass (*Hachonekloa macra* 'Aureola') lights the way up a shady path where golden cutleaf elderberry (*Sambucus racemosa* 'Plumosa Aurea') and 'Baggeson's Gold' shrub honeysuckle (*Lonicera nitida* 'Baggeson's Gold') glimmer at the end of the vista against the green woodland. GARDEN OF VIRGINIA ISRAELIT.

Prima donnas, on the other hand are the showier flowers such as iris, peonies, roses, daylilies, hibiscus and lilies. Larger and often brighter, these are the stars of the flower garden. In a retreat it's especially important to unite these more striking flowers with subtler companions so that a smooth scene emerges. Just as in foliage transitions, to achieve the most harmony, shift very gradually from a large to a medium to a small flower, and from a bright to a medium to a pale-hued flower.

For example, underpin a sumptuous deep pink peony with a skirt of smaller-flowered blue-violet cranesbills *(Geranium ibericum)* and a final edging of pink coral bells *(Heuchera* 'Wendy'). Surround a pastel pink rose such as 'Penelope' with the daintier flowers of a white cranesbill *(Geranium sanguineum* 'Album') and frame the picture with silver *Artemesia canescens.*

In English gardens, rose borders are often underplanted with blue or pink cranesbills and then framed by lavender hedges. This shows the same strategy—the brilliant red and pink attention-grabbing roses benefit from a froth of milder cranesbill flowers and gain unity from long stretches of misty lavender wands. Catmint *(Nepeta x fassenii)* is similarly employed to billow out at the feet of shrub roses. But alas, for those of us who love cats there will be little left but mashed and grazed catmint stubs and extremely ecstatic cats lolling about.

Perennials that drape and weave are especially good for knitting large-flowered prima donnas together. *Geranium* 'Mrs. Kendall Clarke' runs through a bed of old roses, its smoky lavender flowers pulling together maroon 'Tuscany' and velvety red 'Charles de

Mills.' Geranium 'Ann Folkard' sends its wandering stems through nearby blue spiderwort *(Tradescantia virginiana)* and summer asters *(Aster x frikartii),* uniting them in a sparkling magenta embrace.

Lady's mantle also serves myriad unifying purposes. Early in the season its beautifully lobed leaves anchor flower borders in shade or sun. Slowly, flowering stems emerge with long sprays of tiny chartreuse flowers that foam at the base of taller plants and travel through the lower branches as well, hiding knobby rose knees and rising to mingle with the upper layer of neighboring flowers. Small yellow-green flowers of any sort, whether lady's mantle, spurge *(Euphorbia* species) or annual *Nicotiana* 'Limelight,' are excellent for forming a bridge between green-leaved shrubs and larger, brightly colored flowers.

Dainty-leaved, low-growing shrubs that double as ground cover are good melders, too. The small leaves of golden shrub honeysuckle *(Lonicera nitida* 'Baggeson's Gold') are excellent at the front of a warm-toned planting, uniting flowers in shades of yellow, orange and red. Easy to prune and shape to your liking, the stems of 'Baggeson's Gold' make good filler in a bouquet. Its cousin, *Lonicera nitida* 'Silver Beauty,' makes a silvery skirt at the base of cool-toned compositions, say pink and blue hydrangeas, linking them with the cream and pink plumes of astilbes at the front of a shady dell.

At the extreme end of this spectrum from supporting cast to prima donnas are the superstars, those bold, showy flowers that demand stage center

Each 'Elegantissima' shrub dogwood (*Cornus alba* 'Elegantissima') makes a bright accent within the borders, linking the beds with one another and illuminating shady places. In the winter their red stems are equally colorful. GARDEN OF STEFANIE VANCURA.

A slow shift of leaf size makes a harmonious, subtle arrangement; plants weave together to make a unified composition of textures and tones. The large oval hosta leaves meld together with medium-size Corsican hellebore (*Helleborus lividus corsicus*) foliage and blend with the pinwheel leaves of *Helleborus foetidus* 'Wester Flisk.' GARDEN OF BARBARA ASHMUN.

and clash with most other plants. Picture a canna lily such as six-foot-tall 'Pretoria,' flaunting sizzling orange flowers and lush leaves streaked with yellow. Such a superstar requires thoughtful placement and a simple backdrop, for it will inevitably clash with pink, magenta and lavender flowers and certainly will interrupt any gradual flow with a loud "Look at me!" Oriental poppies *(Papaver orientale)* in their original shade of orange-red similarly shout for attention and must be separated from the pink and pink-red peonies that bloom at the same time. It's not only their bright color that's magnetic, it's also the generous size of their

flowers and crepe-papery texture—all combine to make a compelling superstar.

You will have an easier time designing your retreat if you avoid large, bright orange-red flowers, but if you are like me and love all flowers, just place them carefully among related warm-toned yellow and orange flowers. A simple green backdrop or blue companions will also turn down the heat. Joe Ruggiero, a noted interior designer, once said, "I never met a color I didn't like." If you're like Joe, blend the brighter, larger flowers with low-key neighbors to form a tranquil picture.

Another way to look at flowers is to consider them the way a painter would, as dabs of color. You'll begin to notice how their appearance differs depending on how the areas of color are distributed on the plant. For example, many winter- and spring-flowering shrubs are covered with flowers on bare branches. Their leaves unfurl after flowering, so these early bloomers are a blaze of color with no green at all to tone them down. This is a very different look from roses dotted here and there against green leaves, or misty lavender lilacs nestled in among their large green leaves.

Consider the effect of color when the witch hazels bloom in winter—suddenly a burst of enlivening yellow (*Hamamelis mollis* 'Pallida') or muted orange-red (*H. m.* 'Jelena,' *H. m.* 'Diane') covers the bare branches of these wide-spreading trees. Because the flowers are profuse, yet small, the color is moderately bright, and the brightness is muted a bit more since witch hazels are shade-lovers and normally grow where it's dark, beneath a canopy of larger trees.

It seems that many winter-blooming trees and shrubs have modest flowers, perhaps to give us a chance to build up to spring's wild flamboyance. Dawn viburnum (*Viburnum bodnantense* 'Dawn') has small yet plentiful pink flowers that dot the branches like a pink cloud in winter, wafting delicious scent on days when the sun makes a welcome appearance. Wintersweet *(Chimonanthus praecox)* and winter honeysuckle *(Lonicera fragrantissima)* have flowers so small you might pass right by if it weren't for the intoxicating fragrance that lures you to visit the plant as often as possible. The color effect is of a mist of creamy-white flowers, subtle and hazy.

By comparison, picture the effect of saucer magnolias *(Magnolia x soulangiana)* when their gray furry buds explode into enormous pink chalices with so much light and color that it dazzles the eye. Take this a step further with Yulan magnolia *(Magnolia denudata)*. Its pure white flowers glowing all along the dark branches are a truly luminous sight on a spring day. Clear white is the brightest color of all and draws the most attention in the garden.

If you study several white-flowering perennials, you'll see that the amount of space between individual flowers makes all the difference in the resulting intensity of color and light. Evergreen candytuft *(Iberis sempervirens)* with dense columns of white flowers all jammed together, blooms like a flash of blinding white light. On the other hand, bowman's root *(Gillenia trifoliata)*, with tiny star-shaped flowers scattered loosely along the stems, or *Gaura lindheimerii* with

Normally rangy, these lilies and hollyhocks, prima donnas of this border, are cushioned by the blue-green foliage and lacy blooms of plume poppy *(Macleaya cordata)* and the cool-colored wands of *Penstemon* 'Sour Grapes' and *Penstemon* 'Blackbird.' GARDEN OF BARBARA ASHMUN.

wands of small pinkish white flowers, produce a much more misty effect, a lot like baby's breath.

Warm-Colored Flowers

In the Pacific Northwest where I live and garden, we have a love-hate relationship with the rain. It makes our gardens grow lush and stay fresh, but it also dampens our spirits. During the third week of May, not having seen the sun since February, we get cranky. That's when I go out to the garden, rain or not, and cut an armload of 'Westerland' roses. They're the color of a ripe peach, a blend of pink and apricot and yellow, full of warmth and light. The petals have the luminous sheen that you see on tulips, and they feel a bit like satin.

Taller than I am, at least eight feet high, 'Westerland' reblooms several times during the spring and summer. It's a shrub rose, so you don't have to prune it down to twigs every year—just clean out any dead wood, shape it a little and feed it some chicken manure. It may look like a prima donna, but it doesn't act like one.

Don't be afraid of using orange tones in a retreat, just as long as they're not neon. Peach, apricot and melon —all those milder versions of orange—can be uplifting without being brazen. If you want to make the peach tints glow, add some blue or purple iris nearby— Siberian and Japanese iris coincide nicely with the first wave of roses in late spring.

It's easier to avoid orange entirely if you have a small retreat because of the likely clashes with pink, mauve and red. And certainly pastels are more soothing than vivid hues. But it's much more important to pay attention to your own personal response to color than to follow the rules. If orange and bright yellow lift your spirits, be sure to include these colors in your retreat. By nestling them in amid plenty of green foliage and making sure to meld the colors by making gradual

Even though 'Parkdirektor Riggers' rose is super showy and bright red, the chocolate leaves of purple elderberry (*Sambucus* 'Guincho Purple') and *Penstemon* 'Husker Red' unify and anchor the picture. GARDEN OF BARBARA ASHMUN.

transitions between large and small flowers, intense and pale shades, and large and small leaves, you will still be able to orchestrate a relatively restful picture.

Making Bouquets for Inspiration

Arranging flowers is excellent practice for designing a retreat garden. It's a way to learn how to compose a unified picture from a medley of flowers and foliage, how to order the elements into a harmonious whole. The key question in a retreat is how will flowering plants blend together? Harmony and unity are more important than drama. Just as in flower arranging, the individual blossoms and leaves are subservient to the whole picture.

One February afternoon I made a bouquet that almost pleased me, of newly opened 'Tête-a-Tête' daffodils and variegated boxwood to help thicken the bouquet. I love their waxy leaves—small, oval and dark green, with a charming margin of creamy yellow. The petite daffodils looked delightful with the variegated boxwood as far as the colors went. The creamy yellow edges of the boxwood leaves echoed the cream of the daffodil petals, and the deeper yellow trumpets made the bouquet sing. But something was missing. The boxwood was too tall for the daffodils—it was like having a tree and a ground cover beneath it without

any understory shrubs to make a transition. In bouquets, as in garden design, flowers and foliage should flow together into a united composition.

On my next trip out to the garden I spotted some taller daffodils and added them to the bouquet. Perfect! Their larger flowers and greater height put them companionably near the top of the boxwood, so the bouquet began with foliage peeking over the top, large daffodils poised slightly below and smaller daffodils nestled at their base, all dancing together.

If there was one ingredient I would have liked to have added it would have been sprays of tiny yellow or even blue flowers, little dots like a veil—perhaps a few sprigs of witch hazel or winter hazel or forget-me-not. But I had none—only in my imagination could I picture those extra-tiny flowers mixed into the bouquet to further knit the whole arrangement together.

Later in March I looked out the window and saw the possibilities for another bouquet of this same nature. Bishop's hat *(Epimedium x versicolor)* was in full bloom and its sprays of yellow flowers that look like miniature columbines could serve as the filler. Late daffodils and jonquils were still plentiful and 'Apricot

Star-shaped flowers loosely arranged in a globe give the silvery purple flowers of *Allium christophii* a softer look than the densely packed flowers of *Allium* 'Purple Sensation', while blooms of white Jupiter's beard (*Centranthus ruber* 'Alba') offer just enough brightness to enliven this playful composition of pompom-shaped flowers.
GARDEN OF NANI WADDOUPS AND RON WAGNER.

Beauty' tulips had opened by now. I could also add a few stems of chartreuse Mrs. Robb's spurge *(Euphorbia robbiae)* for a little more color and texture.

By June the flower choices were diverse and abundant. There were plenty of large, showy flowers flaunting color and fragrance—pink and red roses, purple and blue iris, pink and white peonies. Beautiful as they were, by themselves they're too much of the same—prima donnas, each vying for attention. Several stems of blue love-in-a-mist *(Nigella)* interspersed between the larger flowers filled the gaps and provided a sense of connection between the distinct parts. The fluffy blue flowers of *Nigella* supported the diverse reds and pinks of the peonies and roses, and linked them to the purple and blue of the irises. A few stems of masterwort *(Astrantia major),* with pink-flushed white flowers, added lacy texture to the bouquet and united the pink and white peonies. I added some pink coral bells to the arrangement—their vibrant, airy wands made the bouquet sparkle.

Flower arranging teaches how to weave individual plants into a unified whole, the basis for designing a harmonious garden. Make bouquets for your pleasure and learn to design your garden retreat in the process.

CHAPTER SEVEN
Structures, furnishings and Ornamentation

We have [sitting] places chosen for

each view, smell or time of day. Up the

orchard under the boughs of the old

pear tree for an unexpected warm day

in May, while the blossom is on the

trees, or on a little stone "shelf"

literally dug into the stream bank so

that with my feet almost in the water,

I can sit excluded from outside sounds

because the rippling of the brook is

dominant.

Mirabel Osler

A Gentle Plea for Chaos

Architectural features give your garden more definition and transform it into an outdoor living space. Garden structures such as arbors and pergolas provide shelter and shade—private places to sit in delicious solitude or to share intimate conversations with a special friend, hideaways to relax and stay cool on a hot summer day, cozy enclosures to gaze at the garden even in the midst of rain. Whether it's an elaborate gazebo or a simple garden arch, structures make a retreat more inviting.

Some of us visualize structures more easily than plants, and can dream up a pergola or an arch quickly. If you're more of a "plants first" person like me, think about designing structures around the needs of pre-existing climbers that need homes. It was like that with my grape arbor.

At first my garden was a flat two-thirds of an acre that looked mostly like a field of tall grasses. Here and there old apple trees with leaning trunks showed promise of bearing fruit some day, after a pruner's firm hand brought them back to productivity. A dozen or

This Victorian-style arbor covered with roses offers shady canopy to the bench below without the detrimental dry root zone that a tree would create. It also serves as a picture frame through which you can appreciate a garden vignette of purple smoke tree, lilies and yellow cape fuchsia. Especially in smaller gardens, a structural canopy is a blessing for the gardener who needs every inch of space for plants. GARDEN OF LUCY AND FRED HARDIMAN.

so grapevines thick as saplings slouched against rusting metal fence posts, their stems trailing all across the ground. A small voice whispered, "This could be a grape arbor," and in my mind's eye I saw plump purple grapes dangling through an overhead support. That image was the beginning of my first garden structure, which has become a major feature of my retreat.

It's very simple, a large rectangle constructed of stout, pressure-treated wooden posts with an overhead wire grid for the grapevines, which weave through and cover it completely by late spring. In early summer the grape leaves are just big enough for rolling dolmades, and I love sharing them with friends who like to cook. Tiny grapes begin forming in June, and these expand all summer until one day in autumn you can smell the delicious perfume of ripe grapes throughout the garden. The pink, purple and white grapes are wonderful for making three colors of juice.

On the south end I pictured a finishing touch— an arch covered with fragrant roses and honeysuckle, with two built-in benches. Once that addition was constructed I sat on the bench and daydreamed about the view from the arbor. The following year I began to plant the beds and borders that would make a beautiful picture to rest your eyes on while sitting comfortably in the shade. In gardens, just as in life, one step leads to the next in a naturally flowing process.

The grape arbor is a cool shelter on the hottest days of summer, the perfect place to sit, either on one of the benches or on a blanket spread on the ground, and share a bottle of wine. It makes me feel as if I'm somewhere in Greece or Italy, on vacation in my own backyard. Just looking at it from my window is a soothing sight—the strong, gray, weathered posts topped by beautiful grape leaves, and the inviting shade beneath it. For a finishing touch I've planted six large terra-cotta pots at the front edge with lilies, heliotrope and chocolate cosmos for extra color and fragrance.

Visitors are drawn to the grape arbor, a tranquil space in the midst of a colorful garden. Friends say it's a very calming place. The gnarled grape trunks give the garden a feeling of age, and the weathered posts look as though they've been there for an eternity. Everyone feels happy to receive boxloads of grapes in the fall, for the vines are abundant and loaded down with fruit enough for everyone.

Siting Your Structure

In deciding where to place an arbor, pergola, gazebo or even a potting shed, think about the structure with its many functions in mind. First consider its use as a beautiful feature to regard from a distance. Like paths and patios, structures are major features in a garden— fixed architectural elements in a landscape of mutable plants—so they should be placed where you want to focus attention year-round. Place them where you are most likely to enjoy viewing them from inside your home, gazing out a window. If you place a hideaway at an outlying part of your retreat, you will get pleasure glimpsing it from time to time as you stroll along a garden path. It will beckon you, a relaxing

These elegant arbors are visible from the first moment that you enter Steve Lamphear's garden retreat, and they become a destination that draws you into the picture. They frame an area beside a pond where chairs wait for you to plop down and relax, perhaps even fall into a deep hypnotic trance as you gaze at the water's reflective surface. A judge for a garden contest actually fell asleep here and said when she awoke: "You won!" GARDEN OF STEPHEN LAMPHEAR.

destination at the end of a journey, drawing you toward it like a magnet.

Structures in the retreat, especially those with built-in benches, are places where we pause to sit and view the garden. Site them with optimal possibilities for picturesque views: an open space ahead with either existing beds and borders or the possibilities for creating them; a soothing view of water, whether an ample pond or the smallest jet; perhaps an outlook toward borrowed scenery of surrounding woodland or distant mountains. You might like to place a structural feature at the furthest end of the garden looking back, or closer to the house and looking out. Just make sure

that there's a feeling of spaciousness up ahead, and not an obscuration such as a fence or dense shrubbery that hems in the viewer. The enclosure of the structure itself will create comfort and intimacy, but the view out should be open and expansive.

Structures clothed or framed with plants blend into the retreat much better than pristine, isolated ones. If the opportunity exists, site your structure within the embrace of preexisting plantings so that it seems as if it's been there forever. In a new garden, you may want to establish vines ahead of construction. Garden designer Margaret de Haas van Dorsser planted several climbing roses even before she built the copper

Heron, beaver, mallard, osprey and muskrat reside at this wildlife refuge and can be quietly observed from the shelter of this moon-viewing pavilion that overlooks an ample pond. Beautiful to look at and beautiful to look from, the pavilion gives protection on a cold winter day when the pond may be frozen, and it provides shade from summer's heat, when the pond offers a cooling atmosphere. GARDEN OF TERRY WELCH.

pergola that frames her secret garden, to get a head start—it takes three years or more for roses to cover a tall structure.

Keep in mind how a structure defines and frames space. If you want to divide your garden into smaller intimate rooms, a pergola may be placed as a see-through wall. The posts and headers suggest a partition, while the empty space within forms a frame that allows glimpses through of adjacent garden rooms. Overhead vines and ground covers below add partial screening and provide opportunities for color, texture and fragrance. In addition to serving as a wall, a per-

gola makes a shady corridor to stroll through or sit beneath in the heat of summer. I've even seen one used to shade a west-facing living room in place of a big tree.

Structures and Furnishings Contribute Style

Just as each home displays a unique architectural style, structural elements within the garden are perfect opportunities to put forth your retreat's style. Even the lines of a trellis may be symmetrically formal or country casual. A wrought-iron bower will have a refined, light appearance, while one made of stout wooden posts will come across as more rustic. It doesn't matter whether plantings or structures come first—the main concern is that they are congruent and unified. Just as a color scheme pulls a retreat together into a harmonious composition, structural elements made of the same materials and designed with a particular style in mind will tie disparate parts of the garden together into an integrated scene.

Your home is a good starting point. If its siding and fences are painted, you will probably want to paint your structures as well, perhaps the same color as your house trim. If your home's siding is stained and fences are weathered, treat your pergola and trelliswork similarly for the most harmonious effect. Repeating the shapes of the house within the garden also results in a unified whole. Echo the roofline of your home in your garden sheds and arbors, repeat the shape of an arched window in a garden arbor, use the same kind of fluted columns for your pergola that also support your porch.

A theme that unifies can be as simple as painting all the retreat's benches the same color as the front porch, as elaborate as designing all the structures to match your home. My garden is less coordinated than I would like because of my mad passion for plants, but the rounded shapes of beds, tables, birdbaths and even greenhouse help unify a diverse retreat.

Structures give a garden retreat its unique style and character just as much as the plant palette does. At Nani Waddoups and Ron Wagner's Moot Pointe you might easily imagine that you're in Thailand or Bali because of the imaginative structures that they built after researching Indonesian architecture. Near

the house, a cooking shelter with a peaked roof made of corrugated metal painted rusty brown is the focal point of The Cooking Garden, which serves as an open air kitchen and dining room. Beneath the shelter sits a huge frog sculpted of clay—his belly is an oven for roasting and baking. Nearby, comfortable chairs are arranged around a circular stone fire pit, with a simple grill inside perched upon bricks. Overhead, a homemade chandelier that Ron built of driftwood, iron hooks and glass bottles provides soft candlelight at night. Big pots filled with tropical-looking elephant ears (*Colocasia species*) and rustling sea oats (*Chasmanthium latifolium*) make this space as cozy as a living room.

Two more similarly peaked rooftops made of the same painted corrugated metal beckon from other garden rooms within Moot Pointe—repeating the pyramidal shape and reddish brown color creates a pleasing rhythm through the retreat. One structure is an elegant chicken house, the central structural element of The Farm which features an enclosed vegetable garden, tidily espaliered fruit trees and meticulously trained caneberries. Thriving tomato vines climb a custom-made set of tall bamboo trellises, which are ornamental even before the tomatoes are planted.

Most breathtaking of all is The Hut, an elevated pavilion that seems to float amid bamboo and fig foliage like a dreamy mirage. It's actually built on sturdy poles, ordinarily used for growing hops, that act as stilts, but the surrounding plants in raised beds cleverly camouflage the bulky underpinning. The same peaked roof unites The Hut with The Cooking Garden and The Farm, yet its ambience is clearly more romantic. Open to the surrounding woodland on all sides, it's screened by tropical-looking accessories: the sheerest curtains made of mosquito netting and bamboo blinds that can be lowered for complete privacy. A wooden Thai couch with thick cushions sits within for lounging and sleeping.

Purple-flowering 'Glasnevin' potato vine (*Solanum crispum* 'Glasnevin') climbs the hut, blooming all summer long like a misty lavender veil. Nearby a fig (*Ficus carica*), a Japanese aralia (*Fatsia japonica*) and an empress tree (*Paulownia tomentosa*) make large-leaved accents suggesting the tropics. They're pruned back hard every year to produce fresh growth with jumbo foliage. Bold-leaved cannas and angel's trumpet *(Datura)*, bamboos with striking foliage (*Sasa palmata, Sasa veitchii)* and hardy fuchsias complete the jungle look.

The Hut is a lovely sight to behold. A rustic ladder built of wood invites you to ascend and enter. Elevated as it is, it commands an aerial view of the garden, a place for the owners to take a well-deserved break and relax, to gaze and admire the fruits of their devoted labor. It may well be the ultimate retreat, a place to daydream or dream, to sit and just be.

Several garden rooms within Moot Pointe feel more like Italian or Greek panoramas, thanks to creatively designed structures and ornaments. These are all in the sunniest parts of the retreat, which encourages the illusion of warm Mediterranean countries and is conducive to plants that thrive in hot climates. The structures here are on a grand scale and feel ancient, as if they were built a long time ago to last forever.

Nani and Ron built the long pergola on the upper lawn out of hops poles treated with copper. To give the structure an old look they finished it with a solution of vinegar and steel wool, which instantly turns new orange cedar an antique gray. Beneath the wisteria-covered pergola, a bench invites you to sit and rest your eyes on a soothing green lawn surrounded by tall ornamental grasses. A distant view, framed by a pair of purple-leaved 'Forest Pansy' redbuds (*Cercis*), overlooks the next two levels of garden, where a clematis allée and an herb garden offer color and fragrance.

Closer to the house a bold, tall pergola in the shape of an arc was built of 4" x 4" posts and 4" x 4" cross-members, with gracefully curved braces that soften the ninety-degree angles. This imposing structure frames a garden room centered on a large stone fountain that you would expect to find in Rome. It's actually a livestock trough camouflaged by stones that were added to the sides, and capped by cement cast pieces. The pergola's arch-shaped openings are like window frames that offer enticing peeks into the surrounding garden rooms. A bust of Sir Walter Scott nestled in Virginia creeper foliage surveys the garden from the top of the structure.

Within this garden room enclosed by the pergola plantings are formal, clipped parterres, in the French style. Evergreen boxwood, *Sedum spurium* and

The Hut invites you to ascend and enjoy an aerial view of the garden from its lofty perch within a natural woodland. Although it's elevated on stout stilts, surrounding shrubs and tropicals camouflage the underpinnings so it fits right into the site like a perfectly set jewel. GARDEN OF NANI WADDOUPS AND RON WAGNER.

You could be in a French or Italian villa sitting inside a formal garden room with patterned beds framed by this tall, bold pergola. The structure separates the parterre from an equally ornamental vegetable garden below. GARDEN OF NANI WADDOUPS AND RON WAGNER.

Euonymus 'Emerald Gaiety' form the permanent patterns, and vibrant red wax begonias are added for hot summer color. Large pots with palm trees suggest a warmer climate.

Adjacent garden rooms in this European-style region, where clearly defined shapes are paramount, sustain a formal look. Sentries of Alberta spruce and boxwoods clipped into green balls guard the edges of crisp beds. Columnar spurges *(Euphorbia characias*

wulfenii) and rounded mounds of purple St. John's wort (*Hypericum* 'Albury Purple') consort with an assortment of pompom-shaped flowering onions (*Allium* species), lily-of-the-Nile *(Agapanthus)* and sea holly *(Eryngium)* that playfully echo each other's circular flowers.

Shapely ornaments anchor the plantings and add to the old-world atmosphere. Graceful urns placed beside the path and a fluted column topped by a gilded globe at the end of a vista suggest antiquity. Folding chairs painted blue sit in pairs here and there to view a vista. They could easily have escaped from a French park.

A clematis allée formed of wooden boxes with pyramidal trellises for the vines to climb adds more geometry to this fanciful blend of Southern European garden whimsy.

Sitting for the Soul

I've never been good at sitting in my garden, and for the first ten years the only place to sit was under the grape arbor on the two built-in benches. If you'd asked me up until a few years ago, I would have said, "I'd rather be weeding." But then I visited Millie Kiggins and Penny Vogel, who sat me down in the shade of an old apple tree for a glass of iced tea. The comfortable, rustic chairs were handmade by the late George Ledbury, with just the right angle for a tired back. Not that I was any better at sitting in their garden than in my own. Views of Mount Hood with sumptuous English roses in the foreground, and vignettes of

This shelter, built in the style of a Japanese guest-waiting hut, is a final destination at the furthest point from the house. It perfectly fits a meditative garden retreat that artfully blends Asian and Pacific Northwest elements. GARDEN OF STEFANIE VANCURA.

hummingbirds darting amid the pokers and penstemons catapulted me out of my chair. What good was sitting when I could be photographing?

But I did purchase four chairs and two side tables from George so that visitors could relax when I held open gardens three times a year. I would watch them out of the corner of my eye, sprawled out luxuriously in the chairs, munching on cookies and sipping lemonade, while I darted here and there answering questions and spelling botanical Latin for enthusiastic new gardeners. I envied them as they sat gazing serenely at wands of pink astilbes and billowing blue hydrangeas, soaking in the beauty. Envy is a good teacher when I stop to listen—it tells me what I long for.

It's taken me years to learn to sit, and I'm still not very good at it. Some shrub in a nearby border looks wilted and cries for help—off I go in search of a hose. A dandelion or spent rose in the distance calls to me and I pop up for just a minute that turns into hours. But recently I made a deal with myself based on something I am just beginning to understand: that I deserve to just be, without working, and that my flowers deserve to be appreciated with pure loving admiration. The flowers benefit from this as much as from watering or fertilizing. I decided to sit for at least ten minutes at the end of the day and just look in quiet communion.

It's a different kind of seeing when I sit this way. I look at the garden with a soft gaze that takes in impressionistic shapes and drifts of colors, with a distant kind of focus that lets weeds and deadheads blur into the bigger picture. I see the slight sway of

Clearly delineated shapes of boxwood clipped into strict walls and balls, columnar spurges and pompom-shaped flowering onions, as well as the blue folding chair, suggest the style of southern European gardens. GARDEN OF NANI WADDOUPS AND RON WAGNER.

giant silver reed grass *(Miscanthus giganteus)* as a breeze stirs through it. I watch the dance of the chickadees as they dart from dogwood tree to feeder, taking quick turns, so much more polite than the pushy jays. For the first time I notice that opalescent blue penstemons are leaning against pearly pink lilies in an affectionate embrace that makes their colors gleam and vibrate with radiance.

Sitting is good for the soul. Every garden needs a place to sit, as simple as a plank of driftwood atop two boulders. Take a lesson from cats, who sit and contemplate on a regular basis, with their tails care-

fully wrapped around their front paws, posed as serenely as sphinxes. Perhaps it was in just such a sitting session that they came up with the idea of seducing us into making them our pampered pets.

To find the best location for seating, take a folding chair with you and try it out in different parts of the garden. Most of us like to sit in the dappled shade of a tree, ideally one with small leaves and without fruit or brittle limbs. Being surprised by an apple on the noggin is not conducive to tranquillity. A hedge, a wall or even a tree trunk behind us makes us feel more secure than sitting out in the open.

In a small garden where you might not want as many trees as benches, you can create instant shade by building an arbor and training a vine overhead. In Margaret Willoughby's delightful new city garden, a seat was nestled into an arbor made of panels of woven curly willow. Any existing arbor is a ready-made invitation for seats. Place your bench perpendicular to the posts if you want the arbor to close off an area, or parallel to the posts if you want to be able to pass through.

Very much like built-in structures, chairs and benches are best situated looking out at a beautiful view—of flowering borders, a winding path, a fountain, perhaps, or a lovely sculpture. Figure out the best angle, just as if you were a photographer framing a scene, and plan to sit where the camera would be.

At the same time, garden furniture is decorative and pleasing to look at, so it's best to place seating

Brian Symes built this bench out of fallen cedar, and its weathered, rustic look makes it seem old and established, as if it has always been part of this country cottage garden. Placed here in the shade of an old apple tree, it's an inviting place to take a break and inhale the fragrance of nearby old roses. Ceramic "Sunbathers" by Katy McFadden lounge in the distant border. GARDEN OF BARBARA ASHMUN.

where it adds to the beauty of the retreat. A bench at the end of a vista creates a destination. Two chairs posed artfully beneath a gnarled flowering plum make an inviting vignette. A large billowing herb border with soothing gray foliage benefits from the anchoring presence of a few wrought-iron chairs.

Two strong tree trunks make a perfect home for a hammock. Just the sight of a hammock is calming. It reminds us of the cradle's bliss, of the luxury of lying still and doing nothing but staring at the sky overhead, at the pattern of leaves, at the way shafts of light stream through the tree canopy. Even a few moments of sweet surrender while floating in a

hammock's swaying embrace can turn an afternoon in the garden into a timeless taste of paradise.

One of the many benefits of places for sitting is the way they direct your view to a particular scene. Bee Smith's garden is full of good examples, because she intentionally set up her garden that way. "When I'm looking out the window, I want to see one thing," Bee explained, as we sat on her sun porch. "I need a kind of simplicity, so I create a whole bunch of centers of interest that can only be seen one at a time." Each vignette is viewed from a different sitting space. "There's a windowseat in the living room, and after the rain I can sit there and watch the moss on the trees sparkle."

Nestled against trees and shrubs, this shaded bench overlooks a calming pond. Variegated sweet flag (*Acorus calamus* 'Variegata') and rodgersia create soothing foliar patters while a red daylily sounds a vibrant note. GARDEN OF STEPHEN LAMPHEAR.

From where we sat in the sun room several pictures could be enjoyed, depending on which way your chair faced. From one seat you could see an arbor covered with purple 'Veilchenblau' roses and a kiwi vine. From another bench you'd see the purple tassels of wisteria.

The simplest outdoor seat was a mossy log that Bee had her husband move to a place in the woods where she watches the deer. "I can sit there for hours, and stay really quiet. That's when they come." The scene is natural woodland that leads down to a creek. Maybe some day she'll develop paths that wind through, but in its twelfth year the garden simply borrows the quiet green woodland foliage for backdrop.

By contrast, an elaborately woven bench was both a sitting place and a sculpture to feast your eyes on. You could sit there and view the island beds with ornamental grasses and sedums, their contrasting lines and textures pleasing throughout the seasons.

For a visual person view is paramount, even from a utility area. When Bee built her potting area out of old recycled fencing, she made sure to create a beautiful scene to enjoy from that vantage point. Standing at the benches, potting up plants, she can gaze over the fence tops and take in the lovely arbor beyond, with her very own blue bottle tree sparkling in the sun.

Handmade Touches

Artful structures and furnishings that are handmade bring a unique character to the garden retreat. Just as you can feel the spirit of the gardener reflected by

The sight of this swing, suspended from the stout limb of a mature pin oak *(Quercus palustris)*, suggests a leisurely summer afternoon when time slows down to the tempo of childhood. In the distance 'Wada's Memory' magnolia turns gold in autumn. GARDEN OF JANE AND JOHN PLATT.

thriving plants, you can sense the same creative energy when it's been poured into handcrafted structures and furnishings. All their beautiful details are a personal expression of love for the retreat.

When you enter Nani Waddoups and Ron Wagner's retreat, Moot Pointe, the first handmade ornament that greets you at the garden gate is the garden's name outlined in pebble mosaic. Right away you smile at the double entendre, at the first of many touches of playfulness that are sprinkled throughout the garden within. You think about the patient sorting of small rocks into separate colors in order to spell out the words, and the careful arranging of the pleasing pattern, and you recognize how much time and devotion went into the making of this garden. This constant attention to details transforms a garden into a retreat.

The pebble-mosaic motif reappears, embedded in the paths and steps of Moot Pointe. It's one of many elements that give it its old world atmosphere, making you feel as if you are in an Italian village or on a Greek island. An ancient-looking stone wall was actually crafted by Nani and Ron out of hand-casted cement rocks and stucco. Ron has also begun to make his own containers by blending cement mix and perlite, and pouring it into a mold made of two large plastic pots that fit inside each other. When it sets up, the resulting material is just soft enough for him to carve interesting patterns on the sides.

Ron fashioned a curlicue trellis inspired by French design, building it first of sturdy rebar. To camouflage the utilitarian but homely rebar, he cut many lengths of woody, flexible Virginia creeper vine and fastened them with wire to the posts and swirling curlicue arch at the top, so that the entire structure appears to be made of vines. This whimsical arbor acts as a lovely frame for The Farm from one side and The Hut from the other.

At The Farm, small pear and apple finials top the posts of a fence used to espalier fruit trees. Ron crunched excelsior into apple and pear shapes, then coated them with colored plaster and sealed them with linseed oil. He constructed leaves and stems from wire and epoxy putty. They were made just for fun, not intended to be permanent, but they actually lasted for four years out in the garden.

Constructing playful details gives a gardener another means to express creative imagination and enchants the visitor. A practical need becomes the means for decorative fun. Ron planted many clematis in huge wooden boxes on both sides of a central path to establish a clematis allée. At first he built tree-shaped rebar trellises within the containers for the clematis to climb and drape over. But it's the finishing touch that catches your eye—at the ends of the rebar Ron added painted wooden balls, so that the tops of the trellises look like wiggly jesters' hats. Many clematis bloom in shades of purple and blue, and a nearby bench and chairs are painted periwinkle blue for unity.

The stout posts supporting the bridge that crosses an entry pond were built first for strength. To make them look less abrupt, Nani topped them with smooth ocean-rounded rocks, and anchored each gray rock to its post with a collar of black rope as a finishing touch. The nautical-looking rope, the beach stones and the posts that might be part of a pier all fit together delightfully. Best of all, when you cross the bridge and touch the smooth, cool, gray rocks that fit right into the palm of your hand, it is tremendously soothing, a lot like the pleasure of gathering stones at the river, or touching a marble sculpture.

One chair nestled into the curve of a quiet green lawn invites peaceful solitude. Sit here in perfect peace and contemplate the beauty of cedar, fir and hemlock.
GARDEN OF TERRY WELCH.

An Artist's Garden: A Study in Rust and Blue

Bee Smith has a thing for rust. Some gardeners love to visit nurseries, but Bee's favorite haunt is a steel yard. "I just like junk," she told me. This is modesty speaking, for when Bee finds junk she transforms it into sculpture. With an eye for form and placement, she incorporates these pieces into her garden as artful accents that support and enhance the plants.

Add to this her love for the color blue—not just any blue but electric cobalt and vivid blue purple, the perfect complement for orange-toned rust. Gentian blue glass bottles, titanium splashes in shades of blue and teal, spindle fences painted blue and purple, a blue table and chairs glimmer here and there throughout the garden, unifying the diverse parts. Blue flowers glow in the island beds—columbine, penstemon, bellflowers, asters, annual morning glory vine—blue for every season. The first time I visited, a clump of bugloss (*Echium vulgare*) radiated an amazing shade of blue-violet. The petals were blue with streaks of pink, like marbled silk. "That just seeded in here, and it's been going for three or four years." Bee has a knack for finding things and things have a way of finding Bee.

A rust and blue sculpture greets you immediately as you enter the garden. It's made of a tall stand the size of a coat rack, intended to hold dozens of welding rods at forty-five-degree angles. Instead, cobalt wine bottles turn it into a blue bottle tree. Opposite, a blue

Found objects abound in this sitting space that looks toward three swirling augers, once used to drill wells. Rusted saw blades rescued from an abandoned sawmill are surrounded by a carpet of Irish moss. The small table beside the chair began its life as a union for a water main. GARDEN OF BEE SMITH.

spindled fence frames the vegetable garden, giving a utilitarian space an elegant touch. "Our kids were tearing out their deck," Bee said, "and I grabbed the spindled part." Nearby a small blue table and chairs sit beneath an arbor embellished with purple spindles.

Whimsy reigns. A derelict fan, with its blades pointed upward like huge petals, perches atop an old sewer connection that serves as a stout pedestal. Together they make a rust-colored flower—a cactus dahlia, perhaps—at the base of the deck. Tuck a candle in the middle if you wish and the long-stemmed flower becomes a torch.

A round, glass-topped rusty table with legs made of mythical creatures is a typical Bee reconstruction. She found it upside down in an abandoned barn, with one leg broken off. Recognizing its possibilities, she salvaged it, repaired the leg and fitted the top with a circle of glass. It was once the stand for an old metal hot-water heater, the kind that sat in long-ago living rooms. Now it gives a touch of antiquity to her relatively new garden.

An old milk can, rusted of course, has been mounted on wheels to serve as a portable market-umbrella stand, so that shade can be brought to any part of the deck as the sun moves. Nearby another small side table turns out to be an old manhole cover

Imagination is the key to interesting structural ornamentation. A welding rod rack and cobalt blue wine bottles have been transformed into a blue bottle tree, satisfying the garden owner's love for saturated blue and unusual sculpture. GARDEN OF BEE SMITH.

sitting on a sewer connector. Bee speeds up the rusting with salt water.

Structural elements give this rambling country garden definite focal points. Two of my favorites have strong vertical lines. A slim arbor is made of rusted posts with overhead crosspieces resembling Slinkies. The pattern of straight, upright lines juxtaposed with the spiraling top creates delightful tension. Not far away three huge rusted augers, once used to drill wells, stand like medieval sentries in the landscape. They have spiral patterns reminiscent of the arbor top, only on a larger scale and moving vertically like gigantic corkscrews. At their base to unite them stands a chaste tree (*Vitex agnus-castus*), which blooms blue later in the summer along with asters and 'Heavenly Blue' annual morning glory.

Stashes of artifacts wait to be incorporated into reconstructions—old gears, a burnt-out hose reel— like so many remnants saved for quilting. At one time Bee learned that a mobile-home court was to be built on her property line, and she imagined that people would be peering into her garden. She began screening the perimeter with trees, but she also joined into the spirit of change by making a suitably humorous piece of sculpture. From an old wheat-cutter and a bed-spring standing on end she made a rusted fence, and she crafted three ceramic heads that perch at the top and snoop.

CHAPTER EIGHT

Plants for All Seasons

The Norwegians have a

pretty and significant word,

opelske, which they use

in speaking of the care of

flowers. It means literally

"loving up," or cherishing

them into health and vigor.

Celia Thaxter

An Island Garden

When you love flowers a lot you watch the buds with tremendous anticipation, checking them daily to see if they're ready to open. You pay attention to their many changes and become as familiar with their early and late stages—spring's bud swells and autumn's ripe seed pods—as with the actual blooms. You take pleasure in the whole process of transformation.

When the first buds of *Hydrangea sargentiana* form in the spring, they look like thick knots of furry gray rope. One day in July, pale lavender petals appear all along the perimeter of each knot. Every day the knot loosens, until little by little a large lacecap flower emerges. The center is a circle of thick mauve chenille, with lavender florets surrounding it like a lace edging.

Other lacecaps are different. One nameless one that came as a slip from a neighbor years ago is an electric shade of blue. The large central part of the flower, as big as a saucer, is made of dozens of tiny blue true flowers that look as glittery as a beaded purse. The edging is similar to Sargent's hydrangea, pale papery sterile flowers that surround the blue center like a lace ribbon.

The tightly packed buds of garlic rise up like so many minarets before bursting open to reveal a globe of silky lavender flowers. Watching the process from bud to bloom to seedpod is part of the pleasure of slowing down in a garden retreat. GARDEN OF MARGARET DE HAAS VAN DORSSER AND MARK GREENFIELD.

'Frank Hunter' daylily starts out as a large grassy tuft. Then long stems spring up with buds at the ends like dozens of tiny fists. These grow and swell, until the flowers unfurl, each a perfect, butter-yellow chalice with ruffled edges. They emit a mild fragrance, just enough to encourage another sniff. Because daylilies bloom for only one day, you have to groom them often if they're to look their best. "There's such a satisfying sound when you snap the old flower off the stem," says my teenage gardening buddy Gavin Younie.

I love to watch the papery buds of garlic as they expand to the bursting point. For a day or so they prepare to detach, sitting atop the flower like a party hat, slightly askew, until finally they pop off and drift to the ground and a round lavender flower head of silky stars is released from captivity. How did it ever fit inside that snug cap?

This process of budding and blooming is more pleasing to most of us than the decline, but the ebbing phase has its fascination too. Roses fade, become papery and drop like confetti. Often seedpods form with interesting shapes and colors. *Paeonia mlokosewitchii,* fondly known as Molly the witch, has seedpods that look like tiny red peppers embedded with black olives that have all been lacquered. Love-in-a-mist *(Nigella damascena)* has round seedpods like little paper lanterns with a bounty of hard black pellets stored inside. It's fun to pop them open and watch the black seeds explode. The garden is full of sound effects and tactile pleasures.

Seeds are released to start the process all over again, and the projectile process is as fascinating as germination. On a hot summer day you can hear the seeds of spurges *(Euphorbia)* catapult like BBs as the pods explode. I like to save seeds for friends in paper bags, and I take pleasure in the variety of little containers that hold next year's blooms. Round poppy pods have seeds that shake out like salt; massive cardoon seedheads with silky tops hide hard round seeds beneath, but you must break into the container with a hammer to avoid getting stabbed by the prickly armor.

The retreat is a place that shows us a small slice of life's cycles that we can observe close up, with all its intriguing details. Inevitably we reflect on the seasons of our own lives and become more in tune with our own cycles of flowering and rest, appreciating and accepting the transformations of each wonderful day.

Put Winter First

Most gardens have plenty of spring color, and not enough winter delight. In selecting plants, it makes more sense to start with winter, the season when we most need a lift, and then consider the remaining seasons.

Winter is often a viewing time, when we may not be outside in the garden but inside our homes looking out onto a scene. Garden designer Stefanie Vancura began planning her own retreat with winter plants; she composed pictures by looking out the windows of her main living areas and using them as the frames. She

would sit on a comfortable chair by the window and stare, visualizing the effect of trees and shrubs with interesting winter bark and blooms, until she was pleased with the arrangement. Only then would she go to the nursery and get the plants. The unity of her retreat testifies to thoughtful plant selection and a good eye for arranging them.

You can do it just the other way around if you're less familiar with the plants, by visiting the nursery at frequent intervals, starting with winter. Meeting the plants face to face, sniffing the fragrant flowers, you will have a chance to see which ones appeal to you aesthetically and emotionally. There's something about the scent of sweet box (*Sarcococca ruscifolia*) that lifts your spirits in the dead of winter. Even though the tiny white flowers are so tightly nestled against the central stems as to be nearly invisible, you must have this plant in your retreat for its soulful fragrance. It's as if the perfume were speaking to you directly, saying, "Take heart, spring will arrive soon."

Looking through books will help too, especially those organized by season. Start with winter and build a framework that gives you plenty of pleasure when

As the buds of *Allium multibulbosum* open, they unfurl a multitude of tiny white stars with green button eyes. Later, even the faded flower heads are decorative. GARDEN OF NANI WADDOUPS AND RON WAGNER.

you most need it. Trees with beautiful bark, needle and broadleaved evergreens, winter flowers and berries will all tide you over until spring bursts forth. For the greatest benefit, place your winter plants where you will most appreciate them—in plain sight of your view windows, near the entry of your home, even along the driveway and at the curb.

How many trees you select depends on the size of your garden and how much shade you desire. For winter, the beautiful trunk of coral bark cherry (*Prunus serrula*) is reason enough to choose it. The bark is polished and gleaming, a deep rich burgundy, so smooth and shiny that you must stroke it. When it peels back, ribbons of curled bark backlit by the winter sun glow with fire, a riveting sight in January.

The white light of Jacquemont's birch (*Betula jacquemontii*) is equally welcome as a serene focal point in the winter landscape. The trunk is a beacon in all seasons, but the entire tree is showiest in winter when the bare white branches make a striking pattern against blue sky.

The smooth trunk of *Stewartia pseudocamellia* is like an abstract watercolor, with patches of muted orange, pewter gray, pale green and camel. The mild colors blend together like painted silk, or a Mondrian painting, soothing and soft, just right for a retreat garden. Small oval leaves cover the branches in spring, white camellia-like flowers bloom in summer amid the leaves, and red foliage color sets the tree on fire in a grand fall finale.

Perhaps you would like some needle evergreens for your winter palette. Korean fir *(Abies koreana)* with a beautiful pattern to the needles that looks woven, makes a striking winter accent. Japanese incense cedar (*Cryptomeria japonica* 'Elegans') is a handsome sight, with bronze tints in its winter foliage. It has an ethereal quality, like soft smoky clouds.

'Blue Ice' cypress (*Cupressus arizonica* 'Blue Ice') has silver-blue needles that make a refreshing sight in all seasons. Similar in hue, white fir *(Abies concolor)* and 'White Mountain' pine (*Pinus strobus* 'White Mountain') both add a radiant touch to the winter garden.

Conifers are best placed where there is room for them to spread their ample branches, so that the entire beauty of form and silhouette may be fully appreciated. Check the height and spread of a mature tree before planting, and allow the space needed. Needle evergreens make wonderful permanent screens and good backdrops for smaller deciduous trees and shrubs that show color on bare branches, from winter's witch hazel to autumn's beauty berry *(Callicarpa bodinieri)*. Keep in mind that they will take up tremendous amounts of moisture from the soil, and underplant with drought-tolerant shrubs and ground covers for long-term compatibility.

nter need not be bleak when the white trunks of Jacquemont's birch illuminate the nter garden. At all seasons the luminous bark is showy, but in winter we notice and preciate it most. GARDEN OF TERRY WELCH. [Inset] Coral bark cherry unus serrula) shows off its mahogany trunk with warm-toned Asiatic lilies, foxtail lily emurus) and yellow *Inula* enhancing its fire. Winter is the season when the gleaming rk catches the sun best, without any leaves to shade out the light. GARDEN OF ARGARET DE HAAS VAN DORSSER AND MARK GREENFIELD.

Return of the Light: Spring

All winter we long for spring and the return of the light. Small promising signs give us hope as the ebullient season draws near. Gray furry buds dot the magnolia branches, and in our mind's eye we see the white satin flowers that will soon be released. Trees and shrubs begin to turn from bundles of sticks into hazy green veils, and the plump buds of rhododendrons and camellias blush with color. The air smells softer, the light stretches earlier and later, and there's a luxurious feeling of days growing longer. There's a great sense of anticipation. All that marvelous flowering is ahead of us, about to begin; all that beauty is on the verge of appearing before our eyes.

Spring is when the life force is most visible. Green shoots push up through the damp earth, green knobs surge out of woody stems, silky cherry blossoms shake themselves out of the tight buds. Sun, rain and wind wake the garden back to life and rouse us to tend, to appreciate, to clear and plant. It is a time of great urgency, when so much must be done all at once— pruning, tilling, sowing. And the light, the moisture, the moving currents of air invigorate us to join in with nature's forces and do our part in making a garden.

Spring is a time of wonder and renewal, when we fall in love again with the beauty of creation. So much life pulsing around us in spring reawakens us to the daily miracles, commands our attention. Our own sap rises, the loveliness around us makes us more tender-hearted. In winter we forget so easily, but spring is the great reminder that earth is a paradise.

What must we have for spring? Flowering cherry and plum, to light up the garden with pink and white clouds that first float along the branches and then drift to the ground like confetti. Japanese crabapple *(Malus grandiflora)* that overnight turns the color of strawberries swirled with ice cream, a dreamy pink.

We must have daphnes with flowers so heartbreakingly fragrant that a few branches in a small vase perfume the whole house. 'Somerset' daphne *(Daphne burkwoodii* 'Somerset'), an upright beauty about four feet tall, and 'Carol Mackie' daphne, a more spreading shrub around three feet tall, are favorites of mine. Lilacs are essential for spring, preferably at least one that's deep purple, another of pale lavender and a pink one, enough to savor in the garden and to cut armloads for the tabletop. Oh, to walk into a room with fresh lilac scent floating on the air.

If at all possible, find a place for at least one doublefile viburnum *(Viburnum plicatum var. tomentosum),* spring's radiant bride, bedecked with pure white lacecap flowers that sit above the branches in parallel tiers. For the full effect of this graceful shrub with widespreading horizontal layers of fresh green leaves and lacy white blossoms, allow at least eight feet of space. 'Mariesii,' 'Shasta' and 'Summer Snowflake' are especially good cultivars.

When the tiny buds covering the Blireiana plum

Earliest of all the cherries to bloom, Whitcomb's cherry (*Prunus subhirtella* 'Whitcombii') strikes a heart-warming note in the February garden, like a pink veil that is a prelude to spring's offerings. GARDEN OF TERRY WELCH.

tree turn burgundy, hinting at the pink flowers within, I know spring is on its way. When the burgundy shoots of peonies pierce the earth, and the ferny leaves of bleeding heart unfold, when autumn fern's bronzy-pink croziers uncurl like party noise-makers, spring has arrived. The garden season has opened when slender spikes of blue grape hyacinth perfume the air and yellow daffodils nod in the rain and wind. What is it that tells you? Drifts of tulips in pink and plum? Make sure to have those plants in your garden retreat to herald the season that all gardeners delight in.

Summer Pleasures

Japanese iris unfolding their blooms are cause for celebration. No garden retreat should be without them. The large sumptuous flowers hold their petals flat, like the open wings of a butterfly. There's something ethereal about the way these blossoms flare out and hover above the stem. The pastel kinds radiate light, and at dusk and on overcast days they seem to glow in the garden—shimmering drifts of blue, pink and whites. The dark purple and burgundy ones are as rich as velvet. Many Japanese iris have fascinating lines and speckles etched into the petals. Some have ruffled edges. Small splashes of yellow at the center of the flower add a touch of brightness, but mostly the colors of Japanese iris are as soothing as cool waters. Their beauty is exceptional and a source of awe. Grow as many as you can find room for.

My favorites are: 'Caprician Butterfly,' white with purple veins and a purple heart; 'Midnight Wine,' a

The pure white radiance of doublefile viburnum (*Viburnum tomentosum*) glows in the spring garden, accompanied by Pacific coast hybrid iris and columbines. GARDEN OF ERNIE AND MARIETTA O'BYRNE.

Opulent Japanese iris (*Iris ensata*) with ruffled edges and fine lines etched in their petals make a luminous splash of lavender in the early summer garden. GARDEN OF BARBARA ASHMUN.

Summer's scents add another dimension to the seasonal elation. One inhalation of a 'Constance Spry' rose and my mood alters. Two inhalations and euphoria settles over me like a silk veil. All that's required to sustain the feeling is an occasional whiff in the course of an afternoon. The fresh, sweet scent goes straight to my head, filling it with lightness and joy. 'Constance Spry' has a very large flower shaped like a peony and packed with petals. The color glows— rich pink with white tints—but the fragrance is what you'll return for. 'Constance Spry' blooms only once, and many gardeners refuse admission to a rose that doesn't flower continuously. But the strength of a once-blooming rose is that for several weeks in spring it puts all its heart and soul into flowering. The intensity of color and fragrance more than make up for the shorter display. Do we abandon wisteria because it only blooms once?

Earliness is also a benefit of old roses. A good month before the modern roses are even thinking of blooming, the heritage roses (those introduced prior to 1867) flaunt their flowers. 'La Vie de Bruxelles,' a pink damask that goes back to 1849, has large, deliciously scented flowers in May and June. When the show is over, I say goodbye by trimming the canes back by about one-third, and look forward to next year.

Fragrant rugosa roses (*Rosa rugosa*) are considered old roses, yet they also rebloom. Their heritage status guarantees toughness and disease resistance, for they were around long before breeders created fussy prima

very deep maroon; 'Electric Rays,' a ruffled violet with vibrant blue rays. But even the least elaborate seedlings that volunteer are gorgeous. Japanese iris are water-loving plants and will bloom best in full sun in an acid soil. They tolerate clay soil, but they'll flourish if the clay is amended with compost and manure.

Peonies, too, usher in summer, some with double flowers packed with petals, and as sumptuous as fluffy petticoats, others single, with the look of a wide-open poppy, and Japanese types with a fancy ruffle at the center of the flower.

donnas. Rugosas also have wonderful bright green crinkled foliage that keeps them attractive between flower flushes and red hips that add to their beauty in fall. Their single pink, white or red-pink flowers with a garnish of yellow stamens at the center attract fat velvety bees. Wickedly thorny canes make them excellent barriers against intruders.

'Blanc Double de Coubert,' a hybrid rugosa, is considered more modern, introduced in 1892, and it is always the first rose to open in my garden. It keeps going well into summer. The double white flowers are showier than the single species, yet the scent is every bit as rosy. I have a sentimental attachment to this rose, for it came to me as a rooted cutting at the end of a shovel, when my friend Loie Benedict saw me coveting her large rose bush. She dug out a runner, wrapped it in wet paper towels and enclosed it in a plastic bag, with firm instructions to plant it the minute I got home. I did, and four years later my plant was as big as hers. Every time I enjoy its sweet scent, I think of Loie.

If I could grow only one rambling rose, it would be 'Veilchenblau.' Veil of blue is what it means, and the small blue-purple flowers that open in huge clusters look just that way. If the color is not enough to make you swoon with pleasure, the fragrance will do it, a lovely fruity aroma that refreshes the early summer air. I grow mine along a fence with trellis-work at the top, and I let it climb up into a plum tree so the flowering canes can cascade down like garlands.

Butterfly bushes *(Buddleia davidii)* go well with shrub roses and I've planted them as a thick screening hedge along the west side of my retreat, where the summer sun encourages them to flower and attract the heavenly swallowtails. Big showy pink, violet and purple panicles adorn butterfly bushes with evocative names like 'Purple Prince,' 'Black Knight' and 'Pink Delight'—there is even a yellow-orange one for novelty's sake, *Buddleia globosa*.

'Gertrude Jekyll' rose blooms repeatedly through the summer with rich pink flowers deliciously scented. Her thorny canes make a good trellis through which 'Gypsy Queen' clematis scrambles; white Jupiter's beard blooms at her feet. GARDEN OF BARBARA ASHMUN.

'Claire Rose' weaves its creamy pink flowers between spikes of vibrant blue delphiniums, while pink Jupiter's beard edges the border. GARDEN OF MILLIE KIGGINS AND PENNY VOGEL.

An astounding maple turns a glowing gold in the autumn garden and lets loose its canopy onto the lawn. GARDEN OF JANE AND JOHN PLATT.

Here's what I love and hate about butterfly bushes. They produce tons of flowers over the course of summer, and the spent ones look dusty compared to the fresh new blooms. To look their best, butterfly bushes ask you to groom them frequently, or they embarrass you with a shabby appearance, so that every time you pass by you say to yourself, I must get over and deadhead those dirty-looking spent blooms right away! But when you do, how they reward you. You stand with the sun warming your hair, perhaps even bleaching it a bit, while all around you the delicious smell of honey emanates from the bush. You might as well be in a bakery. The colors are so gorgeous, saturated purple and violet and lavender and warm pink. Every so often a big yellow butterfly will land on a flower and flit around, looking for the best part, opening and closing its incredibly etched wings.

Fall

As the days grow shorter and the light wanes most gardeners feel a bit melancholy, reluctant to let go of summer's joys, dreading winter's bleakness. Sometimes it's hard to enjoy the bounty of fall, the season of harvest and fullness, knowing that winter is just around the next bend. This is a good time to take a lesson from the cats, who don't think ahead, who live in the moment, who find the sunniest corners and settle in to soak up the sun and revel in autumn's balmy days.

For in autumn the garden is as fully grown as it will get for this year. The plants have woven together into a harmonious tapestry, like friends at a successful party. The ornamental grasses are at their full height and flowering with ivory and pink plumes, and, if you have planned things well, trees and shrubs are showing their autumn tints. Ripe fruit sweetens the air and ornamental berries decorate the retreat.

For fall's sake you must choose at least a few trees and shrubs that will celebrate this season. The tree I most look forward to is the harlequin glory bower tree *(Clerodendrum trichotomum)*, a medium-size tree with many virtues. The large leaves smell just like peanut butter when rubbed, and the flowers emit a piercing sweet scent that wafts clear down the street to entice your neighbors. When the petals fall, fruit forms that looks like a red star with a turquoise button at the center. These hold on long after the leaves drop, making the tree look quite magical. One warning—*Clerodendrum* will sucker and you must dig these volunteers out unless you want a colony. There is usually a waiting list of friends who are happy to have rooted suckers to start their own trees.

Maples and oaks are resplendent in fall. Japanese maple *(Acer palmatum)*, swamp maple *(Acer ginnala)*, red maple *(Acer rubrum)*—take your pick of these moderate-size trees—light up the fall retreat with radiant red leaves that give the garden a warm glow. Scarlet oak *(Quercus coccinea)* is also brilliant if you have the room for a park-size tree. For the smaller garden, kousa dogwood *(Cornus kousa)* is a better size and turns a good red, with strawberry-like fruit too.

Majestic 'Osakazuki' Japanese maple turns the fall garden fiery red, and a nearby laceleaf and a magnolia on the opposite side of the bridge contribute warm gold tones. All this glory is reflected in the surface of the still pond below. GARDEN OF ROBIN HOPPER AND JUDI DYELLE.

If you're looking for a more unusual specimen and can be patient while it grows up, there's nothing quite like a mature sourwood (*Oxydendrum arboreum*), with pendant clusters of cream flowers that look a lot like andromeda, blooming against red fall foliage. *Stewartia monodelpha* also comes into its full glory in autumn, when the vivid red leaves and cinnamon-brown bark make it the center of attention. *Parrotia persica* is known for its interesting trunk with patches of tan and cream bark; in autumn its leaves color up gold and red.

Many handsome shrubs offer foliage tints and fruit to make fall a more interesting season. The attractively shaped leaves of oakleaf hydrangea (*Hydrangea quercifolia*) become all the more noticeable when they've turned vibrant oxblood in autumn. The mahogany leaves and red fruit of the tea viburnum (*Viburnum setigerum*) will catch your eye, as will the European cranberry bush (*Viburnum opulus*). Beautyberry (*Callicarpa bodinieri*) adds its distinctive purple berries to the spectrum, as does porcelain berry vine (*Amelopsis brevipedunculata*), which can be trained along a trellis or threaded through a shrub. Any one of these offers vibrant color to mixed borders.

Common as bread, evergreen heavenly bamboo (*Nandina domestica*) still makes a beautiful feature, with gracefully tapered leaves along the stems and opulent clusters of orange-red berries that hold well into winter. The more exotic Himalayan honeysuckle (*Leycesteria formosa*) proffers dangling clusters of maroon fruit that taste of burnt caramel. Like *Nandina*, it has the look of bamboo with none of the danger, for although its stems are similarly segmented, it stays put.

There are plenty of flowers for the fall garden, and no retreat should be without the windflowers (*Anemone japonica*), pink and white graces that bloom atop sturdy stems. Autumn sedums are plentiful, from the stocky *Sedum spectabile* with thick flowers in pink, coral or white, to the more draping succulents for the edges of paths and walls—*Sedum sieboldii*, *Sedum* 'Vera Jameson' and *Sedum* 'Ruby Glow,' to name just a few. Kaffir lily (*Schizostylis coccinea*), too, comes coral, pink and white, with short spikes of gladiolalike flowers that bloom from August through November. Plant some fall crocus (*Colchicum autumnale*) for their showy waterlilylike flowers.

For shade, hardy fuchsias that begin blooming in midsummer keep going well into fall, with pink, red and white flowers that draw the hummingbirds. And hardy cyclamen (*Cyclamen neapolitanum*) will light up the autumn borders with drifts of ground-hugging magenta and white flowers and silvered leaves that last into winter. By the time their flowers have disappeared, the first blooms of winter's 'Dawn' viburnum should be opening and the show will begin once again.

A FEW LAST THOUGHTS

Often I hear people say, "I can never make my plants blossom like this! What is your secret?" And I answer with one word, "Love."

Celia Thaxter

An Island Garden

When all is said and done, all the information and instructions in the world aren't really enough. You must look to yourself for a few secret ingredients that will make your retreat the special place that you long for. Just like the cook who follows the recipe, but who is inspired at the last moment to sprinkle in a dash of cloves or a smidgen of cumin, you will follow your intuition to come up with the delicious medley of your own special place.

What are the secret ingredients that aren't to be found in nurseries or garden books? Love is the main one. For it is love that will catapult you out of bed on a hot summer day to garden in the early morning air when dew still sparkles on the grass and illuminates the spider webs that float overhead like gossamer curtains. Love will give you the strength to build the soil before you plant so that every shrub has a loamy place to spread its roots. It will keep you out in the garden long after sunset, as you watch a faint sliver of moon make its appearance in the night sky and hear your beloved faintly calling, "Aren't you coming in the house yet?"

In autumn the pleated leaves of doublefile viburnum (*Viburnum plicatum tomentosum*) turn a deep dark red all along the gracefully layered branches. Occasionally a few white lacecap flowers are fooled into thinking it's spring, and bloom amid the fiery foliage. GARDEN OF TERRY WELCH.

Plenty of patience will serve you well. Plants grow at their own pace, especially trees, no matter how much manure and fertilizer we apply. At first they seem to stand completely still, very likely setting down roots and ever so slowly cozying up to their companions. Years might go by while you wait, and then suddenly, it seems, that stick begins to look more like the beautiful canopy you had imagined. Was it really ten years ago that you planted it?

Imagination is essential, for without it you would hardly begin. Staring at a field of weeds in burning sun, you envision how lovely it would be to sit sheltered beneath an arbor, enjoying the dappled play of light and shadows at your feet, the fragrance of honeysuckle drifting overhead. Once you can picture it in your mind, the dream begins to take shape in the real world. Where do ideas come from? They arrive at the most surprising times—just as you look out the window to see if the mailman has pulled up, when your hands are covered in mud out in the garden, while you're taking a shower, or on a walk in the rain.

Unexpected gifts arrive just as surprisingly as ideas. A small packet of seed, a cutting, a potted-up division from a friend. How was I to know that the little slip of summer jasmine that Marianne O'Connor gave me would someday cover an arbor, a delightful embellishment for my entry built by friend Peter Joyes? I had planted the jasmine near the front porch the better to sniff its perfume and to protect it from winter wind. Until the trellis was built, the vine weaved and roamed through nearby shrubs and put up with a lot of pruning. Now it seems that the jasmine and the trellis were made for each other.

I believe that an openness to possibilities is behind all the best retreat gardens. When a friend comes up with an idea that at first seems a bit radical, instead of dismissing it, consider it and see. You may dream up an image that doesn't seem practical, or perhaps another part of your mind is ranting on along these lines: Never, it's too much work, too much money, and besides I don't really need it. Turn down the volume of that noisy judge and listen instead to your own inner desire. Yes, I do really want a pergola, or a greenhouse, or an arbor, and yes, I really like the elaborately carved bench that costs the earth. I'm willing to work for it. It's much more exciting than a new computer.

Pay attention to what gives you peace of mind, to how you feel surrounded by blue, to the small pleasures of everyday life that thrill you. When a chickadee's song restores your soul, find some feeders and keep them filled. If two butterflies circling each other on a first date in your garden tickle you, plant plenty of summer phlox for them to cavort in. Awareness of small details is the main ingredient that will transform the simplest sitting space into a garden retreat. Above all, it's our frame of mind that makes the crucial difference in how we see and how we live.

SUGGESTED READING

Billington, Jill. *Planting Companions*. New York: Stewart, Tabori & Chang, 1997.

Clausen, Ruth Rogers, and Nicolas H. Ekstrom, *Perennials for American Gardens*. New York: Random House, 1989.

Dirr, Michael A. *Dirr's Hardy Trees and Shrubs*. Portland, Oreg.: Timber Press, 1997.

Forestfarm Catalog. Forestfarm, 990 Tetherow Road, Williams, Oreg., 97544-9599. (Written by Ray and Peg Prag.)

Harper, Pamela J. *Color Echoes*. New York: Macmillan, 1994.

Hayward, Gordon. *Garden Paths*. Charlotte, Vt.: Camden House Publishing, 1993.

Heronswood Nursery Ltd Catalog. Heronswood Nursery, 7530 NE 288 Street, Kingston, Wash. 98346. (Written by Dan Hinkley.)

Messervy, Julie Moir. *The Inward Garden*. Boston: Little, Brown, and Company, 1995.

Oliver, Mary. *New and Selected Poems*. Boston: Beacon Press, 1992.

Phillips, Will. *Every Dreamer's Handbook*. New York: Kensington Publishing Corp., 1994.

Sackville-West, Vita. *V. Sackville-West's Garden Book*. New York: Atheneum, 1983.

Thomas, Graham Stuart. *The Graham Stuart Thomas Rose Book*. Portland, Oreg.: Timber Press, 1994.

———. *Ornamental Shrubs, Climbers and Bamboos*. Portland, Oreg.: Timber Press, 1992.

Tripp, Kim E., and J. C. Raulston. *The Year in Trees*. Portland, Oreg.: Timber Press, 1995.

INDEX

INDEX